SALINE DISTRICT LIBRARY

W9-ATQ-034

746.7 Har
Hardy, Sandra.
Handcrafted rugs

WITHDRAWN

Handcrafted
RUGS

Handcrafted RUGS

SANDRA HARDY

GUILD OF MASTER CRAFTSMAN PUBLICATIONS LTD

SALINE DISTRICT LIBRARY
555 N. Maple Road
Saline, MI 48176

AG '02

First published 2001
by Guild of Master Craftsman Publications Ltd
Castle Place, 166 High Street, Lewes
East Sussex BN7 1XU

Copyright © in the work GMC Publications Ltd 2001

Text © Sandra Hardy

Illustrations by Gail Lawther, © GMC Publications

Photographs on page 12 © Christopher Lawther

Photographs on pages ii, iii, 3, 4-5, 6, 17, 24-25, 37, 43,
44, 47, 50, 51, 57, 59, 81, 83, 85, 93, 94, 95, 97, 103, 104,
105, 121, 123, 132-133, 135, 140 by Christine Richardson,
© GMC Publications

Other photography by Anthony Bailey, © GMC Publications

All rights reserved

The right of Sandra Hardy to be identified as the author of this
work has been asserted in accordance with the Copyright
Designs and Patents Act 1988, Sections 77 and 78.

No part of this publication may be photocopied or mechanically
reproduced or stored in a retrieval system without the express
written permission of the copyright owner.

This book is sold subject to the condition that all designs are
copyright and are not for commercial reproduction without
the permission of the designer and copyright owner.

The publishers and author can accept no legal responsibility for
any consequences arising from the application of information,
advice or instructions given in this publication.

Whilst every effort has been made to obtain permission from
the copyright holders for all material used in this book, the
publishers will be pleased to hear from anyone who has not
been appropriately acknowledged, and to make the
correction in future reprints.

A catalogue record for this book is available from
the British Library.

ISBN 1 86108 245 2

Designed and edited by Christopher and Gail Lawther
Cover design by Joyce Chester
Cover photography by Christine Richardson, © GMC Publications
Set in ITC Cheltenham & ITC Stone Sans
Colour origination by Viscan Graphics (Singapore)
Printed in China by Sun Fung Offset Binding Co Ltd

CONTENTS

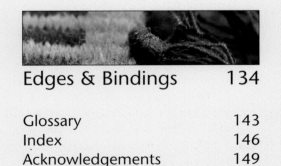

MEASUREMENTS

Although care has been taken to ensure that the imperial measurements are true and accurate, they are only conversions from metric; they have been rounded up or down to the nearest ⅛in or ¹⁄₁₆in, or to the nearest convenient equivalent in cases where the metric measurements are only approximate. When following the projects, use either the metric or the imperial measurements; do not mix units.

About the Book

IN RECENT YEARS the ancient craft of making rugs by hand has enjoyed a revival; rug makers in many different countries are now producing wonderful pieces using both traditional and ultra-modern techniques, tools and designs. However, there are few books which chart recent developments in the rug maker's craft; in this book I've brought together the most popular techniques for creating rugs by hand.

Under each technique the trends and developments in recent years are described, together with information on suitable yarns and materials, and necessary tools and equipment. I also examine the design possibilities and constraints peculiar to each method, and at the end of each section I suggest variations on the basic technique and ideas for your own experimentation. Each techniques section includes working instructions, plus tips on making up and finishing the rugs, with clear explanatory diagrams; throughout the book you will find numerous worked samples so that you can see the finished results of particular methods or variations.

Many rug makers want to work to their own designs, and at the beginning of the book you'll find a section looking at the practical aspects of designing, including tips on style, setting, colour, choosing a suitable technique and transferring your finished design to your base fabric. You can buy many of the materials for rug making ready-prepared, but it can also be very satisfying to dye your own; if you want to experiment, the dyeing section explores the many different methods of colouring fabrics and yarns.

To demonstrate some of the techniques, I've also designed and made up six full-size rugs which are presented as projects. The techniques I've used are **felting**, **needlepoint**, **hooking**, **locker hooking**, **tufting** (or **latch hooking**) and **weaving**. Each project includes full details of the materials needed, working methods and finishing, so you can easily work the rugs shown – or your own adaptations of them.

I hope that, as well as helping you to master the basic working methods of rug making, the samples and suggested variations in the book will encourage you to experiment, and that these experiments in turn will produce exciting and original results.

Rug Making Today

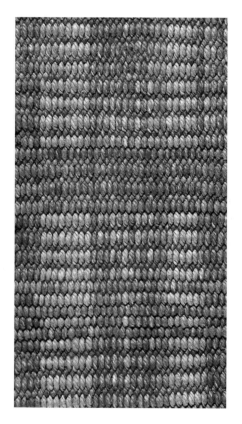

HANDCRAFTED RUGS have come a long way from their tribal beginnings – simple strips of cloth woven on tree branches. The history of rugs has included the 1000 knots per hour of the Middle Eastern workshops, and the functional rag hooking of the early American settlers, but the end of the twentieth century saw a dramatic change away from the purely practical considerations of providing warmth and insulation over cold linoleum, stone and wood floors. Once many homes were centrally heated, rugs became more decorative items, created to enhance their surroundings.

Before the Second World War, rug making was an occupation that many households in Britain and America were involved in. Most popular were the rug making methods that needed little equipment or specialist materials – techniques such as braiding, knitting, hooking and prodding. There was a ready supply of fabric remnants and yarns from the textile and carpet factories, including carpet yarn ends or thrums from mills – readily available in the north of England. 'Novelty' rugs were also a feature of this period, as people began to experiment with different materials; rugs were woven from strips of old inner tubes, or crocheted or knitted from discarded stockings. Felt rugs, similar to the earlier 'penny' rugs (see page 130), were sewn using woollen scraps left over from the millinery trade.

After the Second World War, technical developments in the carpet industry meant that domestic carpeting was more affordable, and as these wall-to-wall carpets became more common, rugs lost not only some of their purpose, but also their appeal and popularity.

Since the late 1960s there has been a growing revival of hand crafts, and a developing appreciation of handcrafted items. Rug design, as an excellent medium for expressing artistic ideas, has been part of this growing enthusiasm for the applied arts. Since the 1980s, design consciousness and awareness has been fuelled by the numerous glossy magazines and television programmes dedicated to interior design, while in Britain the Crafts Council and

Design Council were set up to promote high-quality and innovative individual design. In addition, current environmental concerns have encouraged interest in the rug techniques which use recycled fabrics, yarns and other materials.

Today, rugs are becoming more and more popular in both domestic and commercial settings. In a way they have gone full circle, with an increasing return to non-carpeted floors as stone, marble, ceramic, slate and wood regain popularity. This time round, however, rugs are not made or acquired for warmth and protection, but as interior design features and works of art.

Throughout the twentieth century traditional rugs, such as Persian and Chinese designs, remained popular; others, though, followed quite closely the design movements of the day, from Art Nouveau, Art Deco, Bauhaus and wartime Utility, through to the 60s pop culture and Scandinavian style. More recently, major exhibitions focusing on individuals or specific design movements have created a renewed interest in rugs, together with a flood of adaptations and reinterpretations of traditional styles.

Today, rug design is highly eclectic, making it both exciting and original – especially as many designers come to rug making from different disciplines, such as textiles, fine art, ceramics and sculpture. In handcrafted rugs today we can see minimalist designs, abstract shapes, strong lines and geometric patterns, contrasted with both traditional and more modern representational motifs; the designers are also using mixed techniques, varied textures and innovative materials.

PLANNING & PREPARATION

Designing Rugs

Design considerations

When you're designing a rug, there are several factors that you need to take into consideration. It's important to decide where the rug is to be positioned: how much wear will it receive, and how large is the available floor space? Take a look at both the quantity and the quality of light in the room, and decide too whether the rug will be viewed from one or many directions. Does the rug need to fit in with a particular style in the furniture and the other furnishings; will there be any other strongly patterned items around it? Think too about the age and mood of the room. Once you've done an overview of these factors, it will help you decide on some of the other features of your rug.

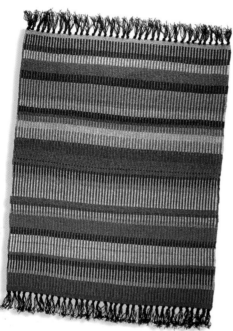

Fig 1.1

Fig 1.2

♦ Size

The rug needs to look in proportion and balanced in the room – neither crammed into a space that's too small, nor floating in a large expanse.

♦ Shape

Depending on the method you choose, your rug can either be a totally regular shape, a basically symmetrical shape with some irregular features, or completely irregular. Regular rugs include ones that are square, rectangular, oval, circular, semicircular, triangular, hexagonal and octagonal. The woven rug (Fig 1.1) is an even rectangle; the felt rug (Fig 1.2) is a basic rectangle with wavy edges created by the felting process. A rug that is completely asymmetrical in shape might be a novelty rug in the shape of an animal or a flower.

♦ Style

Perhaps you want your rug to match an existing mood (for instance, to tie in with a room that has an Oriental or Art Deco theme); or you may want a design that works as a complete contrast – for instance a witty rug in a very sober room or a traditional design in a contemporary setting.

◆ Pattern

When it comes to the design or pattern on your rug, you have a huge variety of styles to choose from. Some of the most obvious categories include floral motifs, geometric or abstract designs, repeating symmetrical patterns, random repeats of motifs, formal designs (with or without a border), pictorial rugs, and naïve or folk-art designs.

◆ Technique

You will also need to consider which technique is the most appropriate one for creating the design you have in mind. Under each individual technique explored in the second part of the book you'll find a section called Design Considerations; this section will help you decide whether that technique suits your design ideas for a particular rug.

◆ Texture

Each technique creates its own unique texture, and the different textures can be varied further by mixing the materials, yarns and stitches used, and by combining that technique with others in the same piece.

◆ Materials

Fabrics and yarns can be shiny or dull, patterned or plain, thick or thin, rough or smooth, natural or synthetic (Fig 1.3). Each type creates a different effect when used for rug making – for instance, a hooked rug made completely from plain cotton fabrics will look very different from the same design interpreted in a mixture of metallic yarns and strips of plastic.

◆ Colour

Pale colours reflect light, and are good for lightening up small, dark rooms; dark colours absorb light. Cold rooms need warm sunny colours, such as reds, oranges, and sunshine yellows, while rooms facing the sun often benefit from cooler colours such as blues, greens or purples.

◆ Durability

The amount of wear and tear you expect your rug to receive will influence your choice of fibres and yarns – and to a lesser degree will also determine the technique you choose.

Fig 1.3

Inspiration

There are so many possible ideas for designs that it's often difficult to decide where to start. Research is invaluable in helping to formulate your ideas, and can take many different forms. You may decide to visit some museums or art galleries, or take a trip round some gardens or historic houses. Art exhibitions can frequently be catalysts for ideas, and of course libraries are excellent sources of inspiration. Look too at other types of creative art and craft: stitched or printed textiles, ceramics, woodcarving, metalwork, furniture; browse through illustrated books on different crafts, watch films, or try listening to music and see what ideas it provokes. Printed stationery, magazines and other people's interior designs can all be inspirational, and don't forget too to look at what other rug designers are currently creating.

The more research you do, and the more varied your sources of inspiration, the more creative and original your designs will be. Make a sketch book or 'mood board' of ideas: include pictures cut or torn out of magazines, photographs, newspaper cuttings, photocopies, drawings, paintings, samples, catalogues, poems, written notes and thoughts – anything which sparks off an idea. You can then refer back to this when you come to designing your rug. Fig 1.4 shows a mood board inspired by Graeco-Roman art, and includes pieces torn from magazines and photographs as well as samples of fabric, braid and thread.

Fig 1.4

While I was writing this book I took a brief look at the work of 20 current rug designers, which revealed an interesting variety of inspirational sources. These included the natural world (such as stars and space, and gardens); children's stories and clothing; church paintings and travels abroad; everyday items such as jewellery and cloth patterns; art movements (for example, Pop Art); and individual experiences in the form of memories, dreams, and whimsical thoughts.

Practical tips

Once you've decided on the size and shape of your rug, make a paper template and draw in the basic design. It's essential to create the pattern full size, so that you can visualize it correctly – especially in its relationship with the surrounding area. For a more realistic effect, add colour to the design using crayons, felt-tip pens or paints.

Fig 1.5

Many people are daunted by 'designing', but you don't need to feel intimidated; remember that design is simply the process of putting ideas down on paper. It's an opportunity to express your individuality, and there's no such thing as a 'right' or 'wrong' design; the most important factor is that the design pleases you and fits in with your surroundings and style.

It's always helpful to make a small sample to practise your chosen technique, like the prodded one (Fig 1.5). It gives you the chance to try out the fabric and yarns on the backing material, familiarize yourself with the tools, play around with colours and learn any necessary stitches or skills. You can experiment with ways of varying the technique or combining it with others, and it also gives you a chance to check your tension as well as being invaluable for estimating the quantities of materials you'll require.

Colour

Fig 1.6

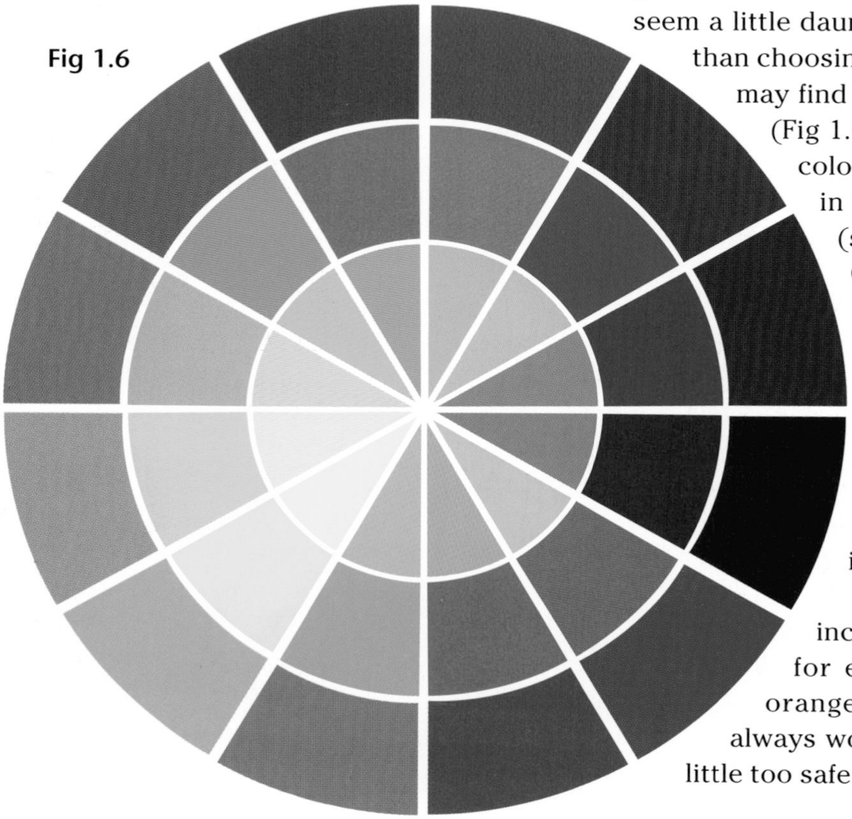

Selecting a colour scheme for such a large project as a rug may seem a little daunting, but really it's no more difficult than choosing a scheme for a smaller project. You may find it useful to refer to the colour wheel (Fig 1.6) to remind yourself of the various colours, with their darker shades (shown in the outer sections) and lighter tints (shown in the centre of the wheel). Obviously, the setting that your rug will be seen in may dictate one or more of the colours you want to use, or may even give you a ready-made colour scheme if you're tying in with other furnishings. Fig 1.7, for example, shows a selection of furnishing fabrics for a living room, and Fig 1.8 is a rug designed to tone in with them.

A **monochromatic** scheme (Fig 1.9) includes shades and tints of one colour; for example, apricot white through to orange and terracotta. This combination always works well, but can sometimes seem a little too safe and predictable.

Fig 1.7

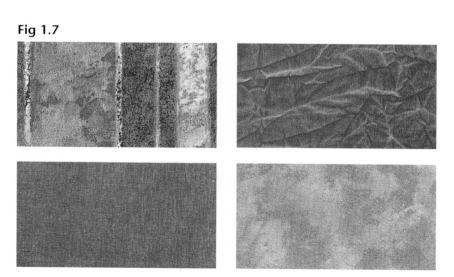

Fig 1.8

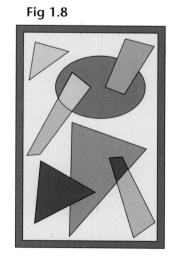

A **complementary** scheme consists of two colours opposite each other on the colour wheel, such as red and green, orange and blue or yellow and purple. This nearly always provides a more exciting combination, as long as one colour is allowed to dominate. Fig 1.10 shows a colour scheme for a rug based on the complementary pair purple and yellow.

An **adjacent** scheme relies on two or three colours next to each other on the wheel, and offers greater scope for producing original and exciting combinations. Fig 1.11 demonstrates a colour scheme based on the adjacent colours of orange, yellow and lime green.

You will also need to think about the tonal contrast of the colours you're using, as colours of the same tonal value become confusing and indistinguishable. Fig 1.12 shows two different colour arrangements based on the complementaries red and green. These colours tend to be very similar in tone if they are used at equal strengths and in equal proportions, and the pattern doesn't come out clearly (a); using the colours in different strengths and proportions (b) creates a much more successful balance.

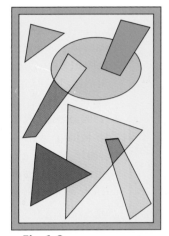

Fig 1.9

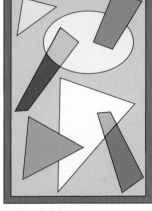

Fig 1.10

Fig 1.11

Fig 1.12a

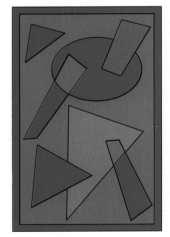

b

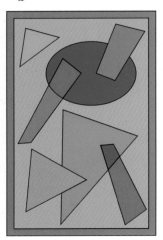

Different fibres, fabrics and yarns have their own individual textures and qualities, and these, of course, will absorb and reflect light in varying quantities. Smooth, shiny fabrics such as nylon, silk and satin reflect light, and therefore appear bright when compared with matt fibres. The duller, more uneven surfaces of cotton, wool and linen absorb more light, and therefore appear darker than shiny fibres.

Nature's palette can always provide a foolproof colour scheme to adopt; when we look carefully at different things in the natural world, particularly flowers and plants, we'll often come across quite surprising, unusual and even unlikely colour combinations. Just look at the exciting colour schemes in the photographs on this page. I painted the colour swatches in Fig 1.13 to show the complete colour range of a red pepper (a), a geranium flower (b), a fuchsia flower (c), and a holly leaf and berry (d).

If you're not confident with colour, draw up several small versions of your rug design, photocopy them, and just try colouring them in in different ways; you'll soon see which colours are working and balancing well, and which scheme creates the effect you're looking for in your finished rug.

Fig 1.13a

b

c   d

Transferring the design

The way in which you convert your original design into a rug depends on the technique you've chosen to work in. With some techniques, such as knitting and crochet, you'll create the design as you create the 'fabric' of the rug. With weaving, it can be useful to put a full-size drawing (known as a 'cartoon') behind the warp threads before you start weaving; this will show you where you need to change or vary the colour or texture. With most of the other techniques, you are working fabric or yarn into some kind of base fabric, and need to transfer the design onto that base in some way before you begin work. First, mark out accurately on the base material the outer lines of the rug, together with the centre point; then add the design. There are various methods of transferring your design accurately, and each has its own merits; some are better suited than others to particular designs and materials. Various methods are described here; use whichever seems likely to work best for your project.

♦ Draw directly onto the base material, hessian or canvas, using a permanent marker pen or crayon.

♦ Draw onto graph paper, then square off the lines, so that each square represents a stitched loop or knot. This creates a detailed chart, rather like the ones used by embroiderers for cross stitch designs; the squares can be coloured in (Fig 1.14), or coded with symbols – use a different symbol for each colour used. This is an ideal method for detailed patterns on some needlepoint rugs, or for latch-hooked rugs.

♦ Tape the drawing, and then the canvas or open-mesh hessian, to a window or over a light source; trace the lines onto the base fabric. If you're using this method, make sure that the lines on your original pattern are heavy so that you can see them easily.

♦ If your base fabric is hessian, one method that often works well is to lay carbon paper face down on the hessian; then place the drawing on top. Use a blunt point, such as a knitting needle, to trace over the lines of the drawing, pressing firmly so that the lines are transferred.

Fig 1.14

♦ Make a tracing of the design, re-trace it on the wrong side with a soft pencil, then place the drawing right side up on the base fabric. Go over the lines again with the pencil, pressing firmly to transfer them to the fabric underneath. This is another method that works particularly well on hessian.

♦ If the shapes of the design are large and uncomplicated, cut them out of paper or card; then lay them on the base fabric and draw around them. This method can be used for any of the techniques requiring hessian or canvas as the base fabric.

♦ Once you've transferred or drawn in the main outlines, paint the details of your design onto the base fabric using acrylic paints (diluted slightly so that the holes in the canvas or hessian don't become clogged).

If you need to enlarge your basic design, use the grid method. Draw a simple grid of squares over your original design (Fig 1.15a), then draw the outline of your finished rug size onto a large piece of paper and divide this shape into the same number of squares (b). Now copy the lines of the design from the small squares into the large squares, enlarging the shapes as you go (c and d).

Fig 1.15a

b

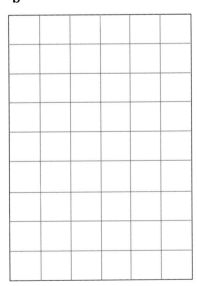

c

d

Dyeing

DYEING CAN BE USED by rug makers in several different ways. First, it's an ideal way of creating specific colours; it's also useful for producing coloured surfaces that are varied in tone and intensity, which adds visual interest to fabrics and yarns. Another use is for over-dyeing fabrics which are unsuitable for use in their undyed state – for instance, where the colours are too garish or clashing, or the printed patterns too dominant.

Natural dyes, derived from vegetables, animals and minerals, have been made for thousands of years, and it was only relatively recently, in the nineteenth century, that chemical or aniline dyes were produced. Many rug makers use these quick and easy commercial dyes, which can be used to create a vast range of colours, both vibrant and muted. An added advantage is that chemical dyes can not only produce specific colours accurately, but can also reproduce them when you want to dye more batches of fabric or yarn to a specific shade. However, there are probably an equal number of contemporary rug makers firmly rooted in the more time-consuming and less predictable process of natural dyeing.

Of the commercially produced dyes, the two easiest types to use are alkaline fibre-reactive cold water dyes and acid dyes. **Fibre-reactive dyes** use an alkali to cause a chemical reaction between the pigment and the fibres; they are generally used for cotton, linen, rayon, viscose and silk. With **acid dyes**, the acid solution fixes the colour; they are used for wool, animal fibres, nylon and brighter silk colours. If you are dyeing a large number of synthetic fabrics (such as polyesters, acetates, acrylics and nylons), which don't take up dye so readily, the most effective way is to use **disperse dyes**. These were developed in the 1920s for colouring synthetic materials; the dye is transferred and fixed by heat. It is possible, though, to colour these fabrics to a lesser degree using the other two types of dye.

Fig 2.1

Preparations for dyeing

To prepare fibres, fabrics and yarns for dyeing, whether they are new or being recycled, wash them first; wind yarns into hanks or skeins. If you are using old garments, remove any seams or zips, and with recycled fabrics cut out worn areas; before dyeing any fabrics, old or new, cut them into appropriately sized pieces to fit your dye-baths.

You always need to take appropriate safety precautions when dyeing. Powdered dyes should not be inhaled or allowed in contact with the skin; always keep one batch of containers and utensils specifically for dyeing, and make sure you don't use them for any other purpose. You must always dispose of dye solutions safely; the manufacturers will provide specific safety instructions and guidelines with their products, so read and follow these carefully.

You also need to estimate roughly how much dye (and other chemicals) you will need to prepare for your materials. This will depend, to some extent, on the yarns or fabrics you're using and the properties of your specific dye, but the following guidelines may be useful.

◆ **For fibre-reactive cold water dyes,** the following amounts will colour approximately 1kg (2¼lb) weight of fabric. Make each solution up in a separate jar or container.

Salt solution: 50g (2oz) salt dissolved in 0.25 litre (½pt) hot water.
Soda solution: 14g (½oz) washing soda dissolved in 100ml (4fl oz) hot water, then diluted in 1 litre (2pt) cold water.
Dye solution: 2 teaspoons of dye powder dissolved in 4 tablespoons of the salt solution, then diluted with 0.75 litre (1½pt) hot water.

◆ **For acid dyes,** approximately 15g (roughly ½oz) of dye will colour 1kg (2¼lb) of fabric to full strength. In addition to the dye powder you will need Glauber's salt (sodium sulphate) and acetic acid (vinegar); the precise amounts required vary with the dye, and you'll find specific guidelines with the dye instructions. Some acid dyes have these ingredients included, and only need to be dissolved in water before being placed in a container over heat.

◆ **For disperse dyes** the easiest forms to use are crayons or paints; draw your design on paper, then transfer it to the fabric by ironing. For larger quantities of fabric the dyes can be bought in powder form, then dissolved and heated to transfer and fix the colour.

Variegated dyeing

Today's rug makers are often more interested in using dyes to produce variations of colour over a fabric or yarn, rather than achieving a completely even shade. This of course creates variety and interest when the dyed material is used for a background area, but also enables the artist to stitch or hook a motif in a more realistic and three-dimensional way. There are many ways of producing exciting, and often unexpected, effects; here are a few suggestions.

Fig 2.2

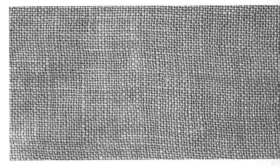

♦ **Dip dyeing** produces a range of shades from light to dark. Remove different batches – or parts – of the material at timed intervals from the dye bath; for a multicoloured effect, several dyes can be used one after the other (Fig 2.1).

♦ **Low-volume immersion,** or **'scrunch' dyeing**, produces a soft, shaded effect (Fig 2.2). Cram the fabric into a jar, then pour on a small quantity of dye. You can use one colour, or small amounts of several different colours; it's best to allow the colours to blend before adding any fixative.

Fig 2.3

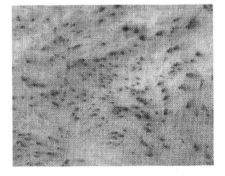

♦ **Spot,** or **salt-shaker, dyeing** creates a speckled or flecked effect (Fig 2.3). Mix the dye powder and salt together, then shake the mixture over the fabric. Alternatively, splash or flick a strong dye solution onto the fabric. For acid dyes, the Glauber's salt should be put into the pan after the fabric, instead of before, and for 'all in one' acid dyes, sprinkle the dye powder straight onto the fabric.

♦ To create **mottling** (Fig 2.4), first wet the fabric, then wring it out, lay it flat, and drop blobs of dye all over the surface. Roll this up tightly and leave it to dry; the wetter the fabric, the more the dye will spread.

Fig 2.4

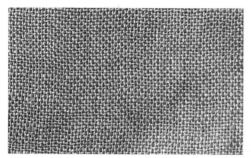

Fig 2.5

♦ **Space dyeing** (Fig 2.5) is achieved by spooning different-coloured dyes over a piece of wet fabric so that the colours gently merge. Alternatively, you can dip the wet fabric into several different dyes.

♦ **Ball dyeing** produces a variegated effect similar to space dyeing. Roll the fabric strips into balls, and part-immerse them in the dye. Then remove them from the first dye and place them in a different colour.

♦ **Over-dyeing** is normally carried out using a single colour of dye on a variety of coloured fabrics, some patterned and some plain; this unifies their colours (Fig 2.6), so they can be used together as a harmonious group. This technique also works well on different-coloured threads (Fig 2.7).

Fig 2.6

Fig 2.7

♦ **Bundle dyeing** uses any two different dyeing methods on the same fabric (or on different types of fabric). This method produces pieces which are close to each other in colour, but with sufficient variation to create light and dark areas in a motif.

♦ **Resist techniques** rely on using something to protect certain parts of the fabric from taking up the dye. Common resists which are painted onto the fabric, then washed or melted out after dyeing, include hot wax (as used for batik), and gutta or cassava paste. Once these resists are removed, the undyed areas can be left as they are (showing the original colour of the fabric), or the whole piece can be over-dyed with a second colour.

Fig 2.8

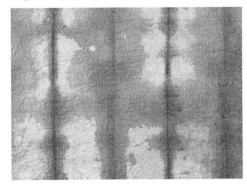

Tie-dyeing is another kind of resist dyeing; this method uses cord, string, thread or elastic bands to bind fabrics and yarns tightly – often in conjunction with twisting, coiling, folding and knotting – so that the bound areas resist the dye (Fig 2.8). The bindings are left in position until the fabric has dried.

Tritik is also a resist technique, using decorative stitching to protect certain parts of the fabric from the dye (Fig 2.9). Different arrangements of stitches produce differing patterns, but all of them depend on the fabric being drawn up so tightly that the dye cannot penetrate the fabric. It's possible to produce very detailed patterns, although it can be very time-consuming to position the stitches initially.

Fig 2.9

♦ **Discharge methods** are dyeing in reverse; you can apply bleach or a special discharge paste to fabric or yarn using any of the dyeing methods, and they will remove the colour in varying degrees (Fig 2.10). However, you must take care not to use too strong a mixture, or to leave the materials soaking in the solution for too long, as the fibres can be damaged and weakened and holes will eventually appear. Rinse the fabric thoroughly after bleaching.

Fig 2.10

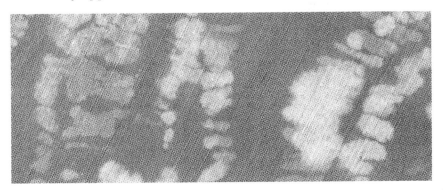

Simple natural dyes

If you'd like to experiment with natural dyes, dyeing with onion skins is one of the easiest methods to try, and produces a particularly lovely range of shades of yellow, gold and burnt orange (Fig 2.11). When you're using natural dyes you generally need a mordant, which fixes the colours of the dye to the fibres; although this isn't strictly necessary for onion skins, using a little alum as a mordant will improve the take-up of the dye and deepen the colour shades. Alum is normally available from larger chemists, although it may have to be ordered in.

Remove the papery brown onion skins from a batch of onions and boil the skins for approximately 30 minutes; allow the mixture to cool, then strain off the dye. Add a small pinch of alum, stir the mixture to dissolve the alum, then add the fabric or yarn. Simmer the mixture for a short time (about 10 minutes), then leave the fabric soaking for up to an hour. As a rough guide, two onion skins in 0.5 litre (1pt) of water will be sufficient to dye two hanks of yarn or 0.5m (½yd) of fabric.

The resulting colour of the fabric or yarn will obviously depend on the number of skins boiled, the length of time you leave the materials soaking, and the type and colour of the fibres. This onion-skin dye not only produces subtle golden shades, but also is ideal for over-dyeing several different-coloured fabrics so they can be used together (see page 20).

Fig 2.11

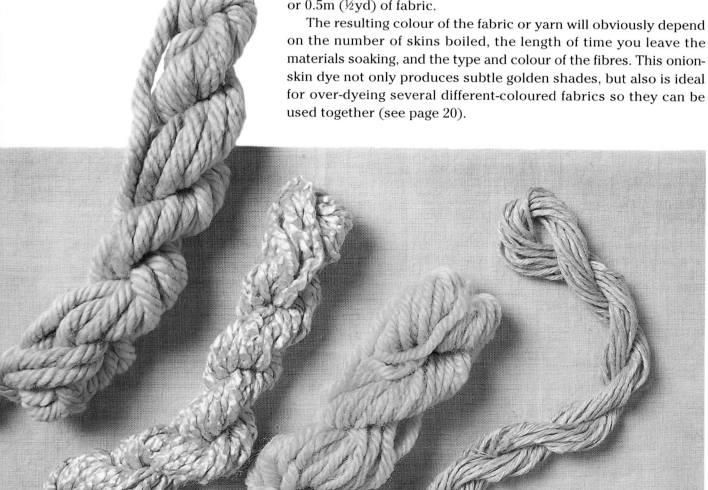

Tea (Fig 2.12) and coffee (Fig 2.13) solutions also produce subtle shades, slightly more brown than the golden colours produced by the onion skins. For dyeing with tea, pour boiling water over several tea bags, add a small quantity of salt solution (see page 18), then add the fabric or yarn; simmer for 20 minutes. Add some soda solution (see page 18), then remove the fabric or yarn and rinse it; leave to dry. For dyeing with coffee, use left-over brewed fresh coffee (not instant!), and boil up with the salt and fabric or yarn. Add the soda before rinsing the fabric or yarn, then leave it to dry.

Fig 2.12   **Fig 2.13**

Keeping records

Whatever type of dye and whichever dyeing method you try, it's always a good idea to keep notes and samples of your experiments for future reference; include both the resounding successes and those which could be improved. Note down the type of dye you were using, plus the quantities of the dye solution and the weight and type of fabric or yarn coloured; stick a sample of the fabric or yarn alongside your notes. This will help you to improve your dyeing skills, and also help you to reproduce particular effects as closely as possible when you need to.

TECHNIQUES & PROJECTS

Braided Rugs

BRAIDS, OR PLAITS, were first made by the ancient Egyptians as long ago as 6000 BC, and can be discovered in the decorative art of many different cultures. In the mid-nineteenth century, braiding became popular with the early American settlers, making use of recycled fabrics – mostly clothing – to create rugs to cover and decorate bare floors. In Britain braided rugs were very much part of the 'make do and mend' way of life during the Second World War.

In many British people's minds, braided rugs haven't really moved on dramatically since those early times of hardship. This is probably partly because of their limited design possibilities, and perhaps partly because of their association with times of austerity. Contemporary rug designers have tended to use braiding only in conjunction with other techniques. However, in America, braided rugs and mats are very popular; pre-folded wool or cotton strips are sold for people making their own rugs, and commercially there are many braided rugs for sale, created using braiding machines.

Materials

No base fabric (e.g. canvas or hessian) is needed for this technique, as the braids are sewn together to create the rug. You may, however, want to back the finished rug with fabric. The braids themselves can be made from a variety of fabrics, new or old, such as wool (Fig 3.1), cotton, felt (Fig 3.2a and b), velvet, corduroy, tweed, nylon, tights (pantyhose; Fig 3.3), jute and plastic. You can also use single thick yarns, or combined thinner yarns and fleece – and, for a more experimental effect, try cords, grasses and rope.

A combination of different materials provides textural interest, but you need to ensure that you use similar thicknesses for each part of the braid; otherwise the braids will be uneven and bumpy, and won't lie flat on the floor. Thinner fabric can be padded out with polyester wadding, folding the raw edges over a narrow strip of the wadding, creating a very soft and spongy mat. It's best to avoid fabrics that unravel or fray dramatically, although fraying can be controlled to some extent if you're using the 'turning-in' method (see page 31) for the strips.

All fabric should be cut on the straight grain. The width of the strips will depend on the thickness and size of braid you require, but an average width is 5–7.5cm (2–3in). Cut the strips as long as possible, as roughly one third of the length will be lost in the braiding. Once you've decided on the design of the rug and made a sample braid, you'll be able to estimate the length of the strips necessary to create the different braids. If you do need to join fabric strips, do this before you begin braiding, using a cross-way seam (see page 31). Try to stagger these joins along the length of the braid, to avoid creating a lump or bulge.

Fig 3.1

Fig 3.2a

Fig 3.2b

Equipment and tools

No tools are necessary for this technique, although a number of large safety pins are invaluable for holding the ends of the braids. A strip cutting machine (as used for prodded rugs, see page 67) can be useful for creating the fabric strips, though not all cutters are suitable; although many have interchangeable blades, their maximum cutting width may still be too narrow.

Fig 3.4

One of the reasons that braided rugs are particularly popular in America is the introduction of a simple tool for turning under the edges of fabric strips (Fig 3.4), developed about 50 years ago. The turning is done as the strip is being braided rather than beforehand, so you require three tools for a three-strand braid.

Fig 3.3

Design considerations

♦ The main design possibilities using this technique focus on colour, the textures of the fabrics and yarns used, and the ways in which different braids are combined to create designs. You can work the colour scheme out carefully beforehand, using a variety of light and dark, patterned and plain fabrics.

♦ You can produce subtle changes in the design by altering one strand of the braid at a time. In contrast to this gradual movement of colours, dramatic changes can be made by introducing bold and bright colours. Alternatively, you can adopt the 'hit and miss' method, where colours and fabrics are placed randomly together.

♦ One particularly interesting effect involves using fabrics of different types but similar weights, such as cotton, velvet and lurex, in the same colour; this highlights their individual textures. Another option is to select a variety of fabrics (again of similar weight), patterned and plain, and over-dye them (see page 20), using a medium colour; the harmonizing dye means that the different fabrics co-ordinate, but their original patterns are still evident through the colour.

♦ The arrangement of the braids can create its own pattern; gentle manoeuvring around curves (Fig 3.5) is far more successful than acute angles.

Fig 3.5

Working instructions

If you're using fabric strips with unturned edges, then you can expect some fraying to be visible on the finished rug – unless, of course, you're using a non-fray fabric such as felt or suede. It creates a better finish if you fold the raw edges of the strips under; these can be ironed in place, or tacked or machine stitched. If you use folding tools (shown on page 29), the folding is done while you are braiding.

To start a braid, join the ends of three fabric strips in a 'T' shape so that all the raw edges are enclosed (Fig 3.6). Secure this with a safety pin and attach the pin to a hook in the wall, so that you can pull against the hook to create an even tension while you're braiding. Make the braid by folding first a right-hand strip across to the centre (Fig 3.7a), then a left-hand strip (b), and so on in the same way. As you work, make sure that you position any joins in the strips on the underside of the braid. When the braiding is complete, secure the final ends with another safety pin to prevent them unravelling.

Shape the braid into the required pattern by pinning it, then lace the edges together (Fig 3.8). Taper the last 15–25cm (6–10in) by trimming the strips (Fig 3.9) and then braiding to the end. Sew this tapered section to its adjacent braid, tuck each tail into a loop on a neighbouring braid, and finally sew the ends securely (Fig 3.10).

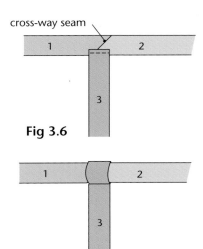

cross-way seam

Fig 3.6

Fig 3.7a 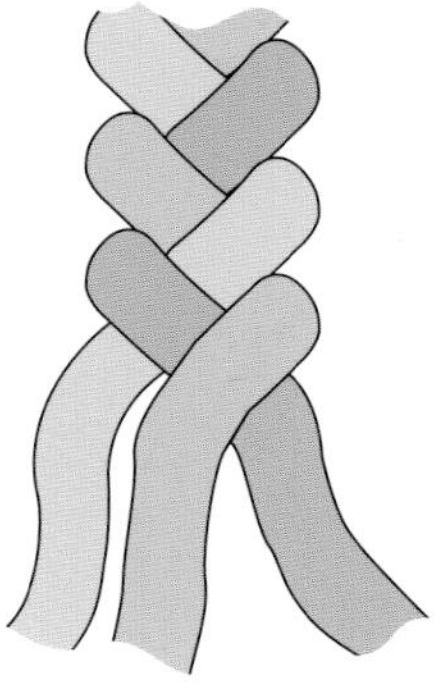   **b**

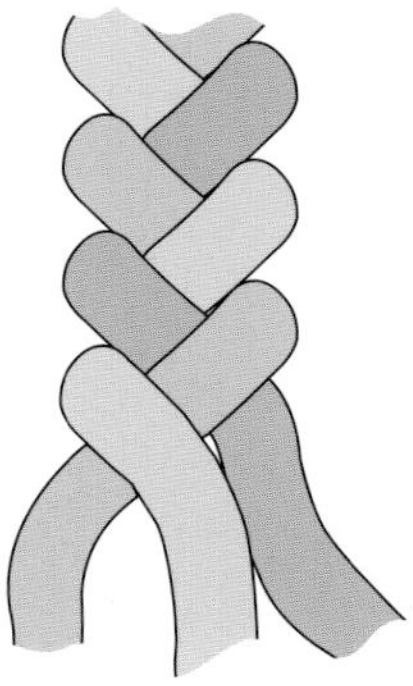

right side   right side

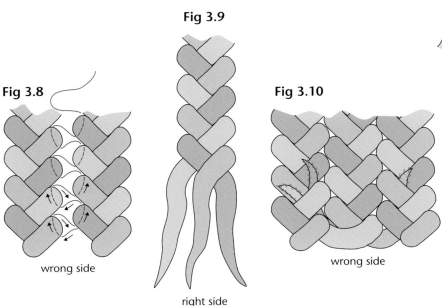

Fig 3.9

Fig 3.8

Fig 3.10

wrong side

right side

wrong side

Finishing

If you've made your rug by coiling the braids around each other, it won't require any further finishing apart from a backing. However, where a rug has the braid ends showing, as in a square or rectangular shape, these will need securing and tidying. The easiest method is simply to stitch across the braids at the required level by hand or machine, leaving the braid ends to be unravelled as a fringe, as in the blue sample on the opposite page. Alternatively, bind the edges of the braids with a strip of fabric, either leaving part of it visible on the front as a decorative edge or turning it completely to the wrong side like a facing (Fig 3.11).

Fig 3.11

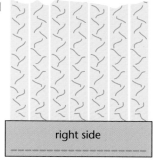
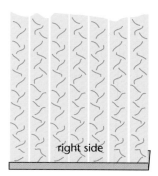

It's advisable to add a backing to finished braided rugs; use a strong cotton fabric, such as platform cloth, or a fine hessian, for added protection. Slip-stitch the backing in place with a strong linen thread; this is easier if you use a curved needle.

Variations

The basic three-strand braid can be extended to include four, five or more strands (Fig 3.12), up to a maximum of 12. These wider braids aren't as flexible as ordinary braids, and are much bulkier, so they can't easily be formed into curves. The best use for wider braids is to create rectangular rugs in strips; you could use the ends to form fringes.

Try novelty-dyed fabrics or yarns, either bought ready-coloured or dyed yourself.

Combine braiding with another technique, for instance as a border or surface decoration combined with hooking, to maximize the differences in pile and texture.

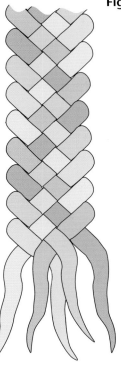

Fig 3.12

Felt Rugs

FELTING IS THE PROCESS of unifying several layers of fibre to create a thick, soft fabric; it's a technique which is often used for furnishing and clothing fabrics, and can also be used to create rugs. Felt making is an ancient craft, and is found in the craft traditions of many different regions of the world; it's thought to have been introduced into my homeland, Britain, during Roman times. Today there is a renewed interest in felted fabrics – in fashion, as a foundation for embroidery, and for use as an interior furnishing. No doubt one reason for the increasing popularity of felt is its versatility; the way the material is produced enables the felt maker to produce an amazing range of textures, shapes and thicknesses.

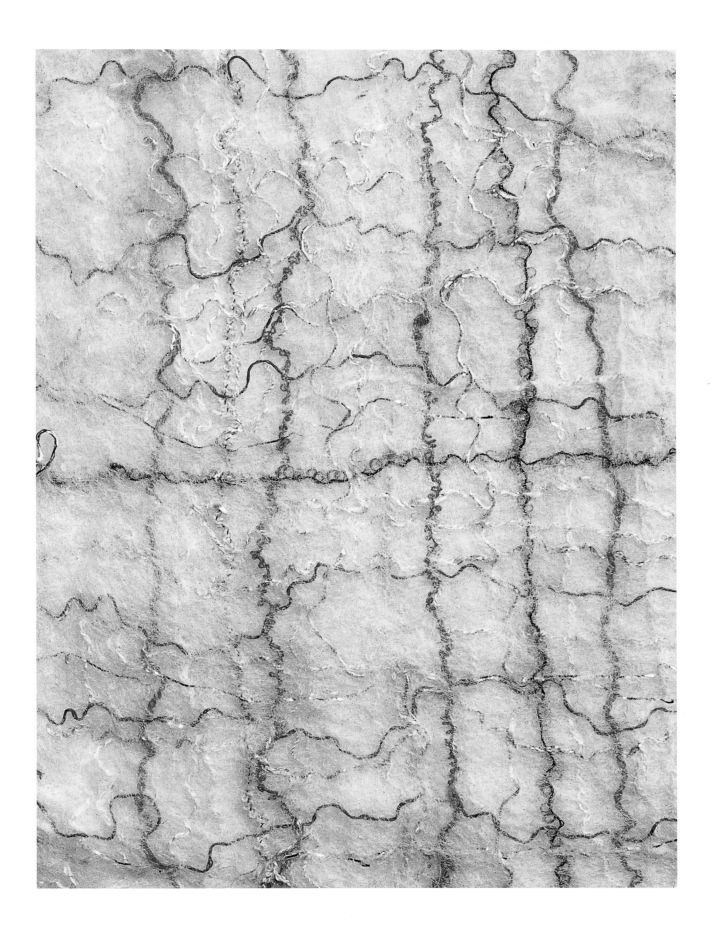

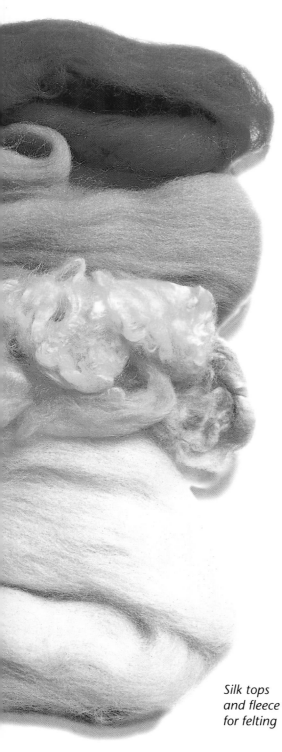

*Silk tops
and fleece
for felting*

Materials

Felt is made from fleece – that is, wool shorn from sheep. Fleece can be bought untreated (often as a whole fleece), or ready to use. If the fleece is bought in its natural state, it will need washing and scouring, and you will have to remove any debris it contains; you will then need to card it (comb it to remove knots and tangles). If it's bought ready-prepared, then it will have already been carded but will require teasing out into a uniform thickness. Ready-prepared fleece can also be bought as combed tops; these have the fibres lying parallel to each other, and are ready-dyed.

Fleece varies a great deal in the length and coarseness of its fibres; for felt making, it's important to select a short-staple fleece (one with short fibres), and one which is not too coarse. Fibres are also graded, and one below a 56 count will not felt easily. As a rough estimate, approximately 1.5–2kg (3–4½lb) of wool will be sufficient to make a 70 x 100cm (30 x 40in) rug.

Equipment and tools

To make felt you will need several pieces of simple equipment:

♦ a thin rush or reed mat, at least the size of your proposed rug
♦ a piece of thin cotton, muslin or net, twice the length of your proposed rug and slightly wider
♦ liquid detergent (washing-up liquid) or household soap
♦ rubber gloves
♦ a polythene sheet
♦ if you're working with an unprepared fleece, you'll also need a pair of carders or a drum carder. Hand carders are rectangular pieces of wood with handles; one side of each carder is covered with fine steel pins. A drum carder has two rollers covered with similar pins; these are rotated against each other by turning a handle.

Design considerations

♦ Felt making is not suitable for creating rugs with very detailed or intricate patterns, unless these are stitched into the felt after the rug has been made. It's better suited to larger-scale designs – simple shapes or bold motifs with vague outlines.

♦ The slight unpredictability of how the coloured fibres will behave, as they bond with each other and the background, is part of the excitement of felt making.

♦ A rich depth of colour is also one of the appealing properties of felt, created by building up layers of fibre in different shades (Fig 4.1); this depth makes felt quite unlike any of the other methods of creating rugs.

♦ The textural quality of felt is an obvious design element, especially when different fleeces are mixed and other fibres are introduced – for instance, the fluffiness of angora and mohair, or the lustrous quality of silk. There are numerous ways in which you can vary the textural qualities of the finished piece by incorporating fabrics, threads and other objects under the final layer of fleece before felting. Once you've created the felt there are many ways in which you can decorate the surface, using anything from straightforward quilting patterns through to more intricate free machine embroidery, hand stitching or appliqué.

Fig 4.1

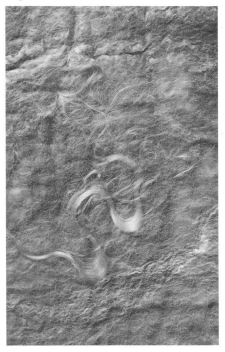

Working instructions

For a rug of medium thickness, you will need to lay down approximately ten layers of fibre. The extent of the felting necessary – that is, the amount of time you need to spend working the fibres together – will depend on the amount of wear and tear the rug is likely to receive.

Cover your working surface with polythene sheeting to protect it. Lay the reed matting flat and place the piece of muslin or net over the matting (Fig 4.2). Tease out the first batch of fibres, laying them down so that the fibres all lie in one direction, and cover the area of your rug well (Fig 4.3).

Fig 4.2

Fig 4.3

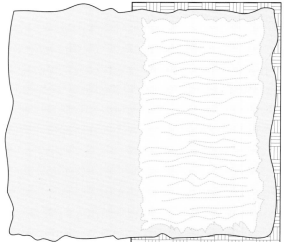

Remember that there will be some shrinkage as the rug is felted, so allow for that as you put down the first layer. If you are using combed tops, then you will need to alternate the direction of the fibres in each layer; lay the second batch of fibres at 90° to the first (Fig 4.4), and so on. (If you are using carded wool, the fibres have already been mixed in all directions.)

When you have completed ten layers of fibre, fold the other half of the muslin or net over to cover the final layer (Fig 4.5), and loosely tack the materials together. For the felting itself, work on a well-protected surface – either a worktop or table or, if you find it easier, the floor.

Start by pouring boiling water in the centre of the rug; put on the rubber gloves, and work several squirts of liquid soap into the water-soaked fibres using a gentle rubbing motion. Continue working outwards, from the centre of the rug right to the edges, adding more boiling water and soap as you go.

Press out the cooling water and repeat the process with more boiling water and soap, rubbing more vigorously this time.

After 15–20 minutes of rubbing, lift the muslin or net to see if the fibres have matted together and no longer slip out of position. If they still move, continue the felting process until they bond.

When the fibres have stopped slipping, remove the muslin or net cover, roll the rug up in the matting, and roll the whole bundle backwards and forwards. Keep doing this for at least 30 minutes. You can speed up this final part of the felting by squeezing out the cooling water and adding more boiling water; then re-roll the bundle and continue rolling it to and fro until some shrinkage has occurred and all the fibres of the rug are felted – that is, bonded into one layer.

Fig 4.4

Finishing

Once the felt has dried no further finishing is required.

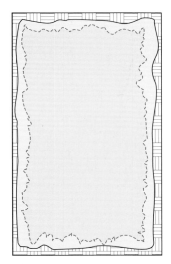

Fig 4.5

Fig 4.6

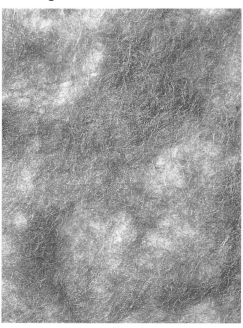

Variations

You can create a rug with curly edges by using longer staple lengths, e.g. a long wool mix of Wensleydale, Teeswater and Massam fleece (48 count and roughly 25cm (10in) length) or North Leicester (48/50 count and 23–25cm (9-10in) length). During the felting process you need to pull these fringes out from the main rug several times.

Carding two or more colours of fibre together (combing them between toothed surfaces) creates a mottled effect (Fig 4.6).

For textural variety, add different materials to the penultimate layer; in this way they will be thoroughly trapped by the fleece fibres, but still visible (Figs 4.7 and 4.8). Try silk and metallic threads, fancy synthetic yarns, feathers, raffia, etc.

You can also place pieces of fabric, weaving, knitting and embroidery under the top layer. If you use firm fabric or pieces of weaving, remove some of the warp and weft threads to allow the fleece fibres to work through the gaps and integrate the pieces into the felting. When the felting process is completed these added pieces may pucker, creating a unique texture which you can exploit as a design feature (Fig 4.9).

Fig 4.7

Fig 4.8

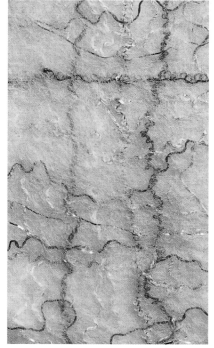

Try including hair and wool from other animals (such as angora, mohair, camel, cashmere, llama, alpaca) in the layering process; they will then be built into the felt.

Cut pieces of handmade felt into patterns and lay them on top of the prepared fibres; the shapes will then become bonded onto the surface (Fig 4.10).

Fig 4.9

Fig 4.10

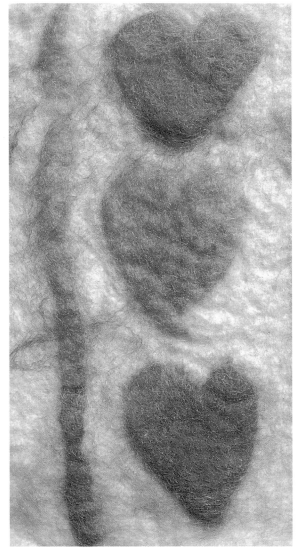

FELT PROJECT
Cream Panelled Rug

MATERIALS
- 1.5kg (3lb) of undyed fine wool top (64s, 12cm (4½in) staple)
- dyed fine wool top: 10g (⅓oz) magenta, 60g (2½oz) baby pink
- a small quantity of dyed mulberry silk top (you can dye this yourself, or use ready-dyed tops)
- a small quantity of angora fur
- a piece of muslin or net, approximately 200 x 135cm (80 x 55in)
- reed or straw matting, larger than your finished rug size
- soap (a bar, or washing-up liquid)
- a polythene sheet, approximately 110 x 150cm (44 x 59in)

This is a comparatively quick rug to make. The main part of the rug uses natural-coloured fleece, and the surface is decorated with panels of pre-dyed wool tops mixed with hand-dyed silk tops and a little angora. The felting process ensures that the various decorative fibres are incorporated well into the main body of the rug. Different types of wool fibre have varying shrinkage rates, so it's advisable to make a sample first using your chosen fibres; as a guide, the overall shrink-age of this rug was approximately 10%.

FINISHED SIZE: 79 x 104cm (31 x 41in)

Working instructions

DYEING
If the silk tops are bought undyed, use acid dyes to colour them.

MAKING THE FELT
Lay the polythene sheet on a flat surface and lay the matting on top; place the piece of muslin or net over the matting.

Begin by teasing the undyed wool top apart to create pieces of two different lengths: roughly 85cm (33in) and 125cm (50in). To create the first layer, lay some of the longer pieces down on the muslin or net, side by side, spreading the fibres of each piece out to a width of approximately 15cm (6in). Now create the second layer by laying some of the shorter pieces in the opposite direction, so that the fibres are lying at 90° to those underneath (see page 45).

Continue layering until you have completed ten layers; try to keep the edges of the rug shape level and the overall shape rectangular. (If you have access to an open frame, slightly larger than the planned rug, this is ideal for laying the fibres inside and will ensure parallel sides and right-angled corners.)

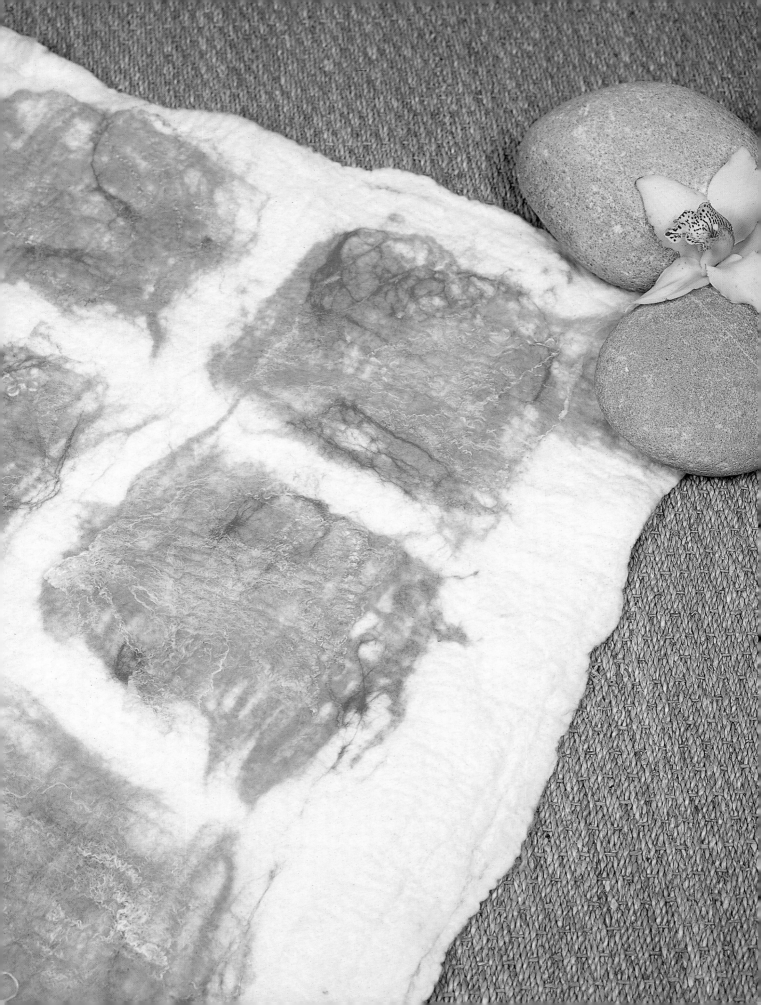

Next, create the rectangular coloured panels. Tease the pink dyed wool tops out into thin layers and use them to create nine panels on the rug, each measuring roughly 18 x 28cm (7 x 11in); make each one in two layers, one with the fibres going lengthwise, and one with them going widthways (Fig 4.11). Position each panel approximately 10–15cm (4–6in) from the edges, and leave gaps of roughly 6cm (2¼in) between the panels.

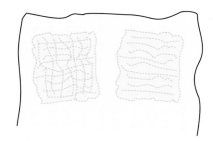

Fig 4.11

Now pull apart the orange and yellow dyed silk tops, and apply these randomly over the decorative panels; do the same with the angora and the magenta wool tops (Fig 4.12). Try to make the edges of these rectangular panels very irregular, with wisps of colours trailing into the undyed fleece around. When you're satisfied with the arrangement of the panels, cover the top of the work with the other half of the muslin or net, taking care not to disturb the loose fibres. (If you used a frame, remove this before covering with the muslin.) Tacking the layers together is optional, but it does help to hold everything together – as long as you can make the stitches without disturbing the work too much.

Fig 4.12

Pour boiling water onto the centre area of the rug, and apply the soap. Carefully start rubbing, then gradually add more hot water and soap, moving out to the edges of the rug. Now repeat the process, rubbing the whole area more vigorously, until the fibres have matted together.

Remove the muslin or net and, if necessary, tug at the edges of the matted fibres to straighten them. Roll the matted fibres in the reed mat, and then wrap the muslin around the outside. Squeeze out excess water, then roll the rug back and forth vigorously. Continue unwrapping, adding boiling water, re-wrapping, squeezing and re-rolling. This may take some time because of the thickness of the fibres, but eventually the fibres will be completely felted.

FINISHING

Once the felting process is complete, you can spin-dry the rug or leave it to dry naturally. No extra finishing is necessary, but if you wish you can decorate the rug with embroidery at this stage, and you could add a backing fabric for extra durability.

Needlepoint Rugs

NEEDLEPOINT RUGS began their popularity several centuries ago; during the sixteenth century large, magnificent table carpets were being stitched, examples of which can be seen in the Victoria and Albert Museum, London. After that time needlepoint items became progressively smaller and finer, and by the nineteenth century, with the introduction of Berlin woolwork with its chemically dyed wools and readily available charts, every item imaginable began to be decorated with needlepoint designs.

Along with many other embroidery and craft techniques, needlepoint has enjoyed a general revival of interest since the Second World War. It increased in popularity particularly during the 1970s and 1980s, inspired by Kaffe Fassett's striking contemporary designs, along with Elisabeth Bradley's traditional Victorian pictures and Beth Russell's interpretations of the work of William Morris.

In common with many other stitching techniques, needlepoint is time-consuming and therefore expensive to produce. This has meant that most designs appear in pattern or kit form, to be stitched by the purchaser. However, the 'needlepoint look' is still very popular, as we can see from the large number of commercially woven imitations, and the import of needlepoint rugs, carpets and cushions stitched in non-industrialized countries.

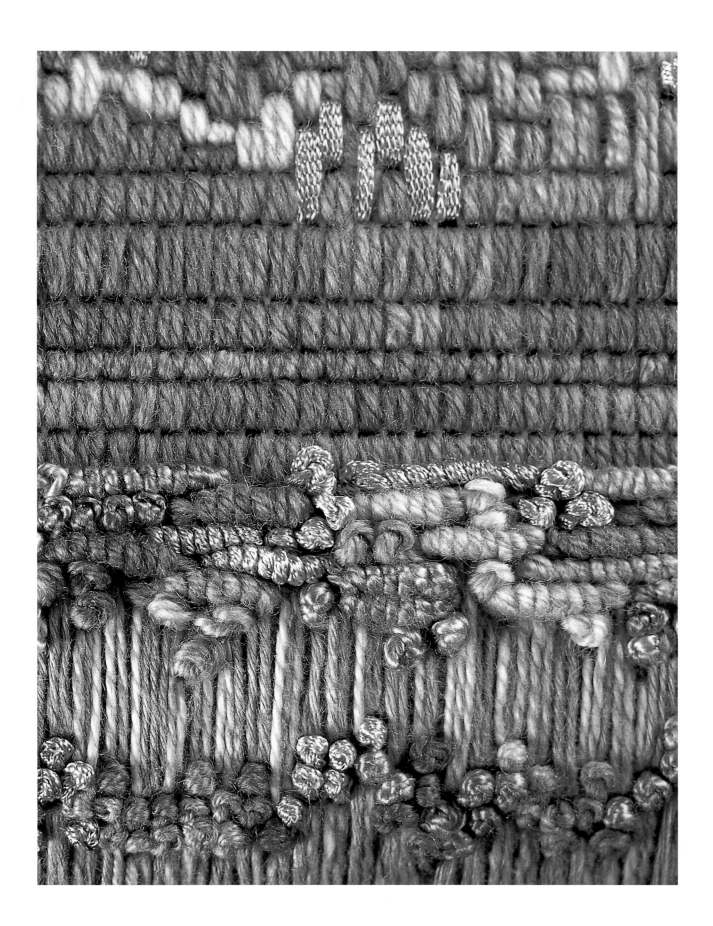

Materials and yarns

Unlike woven rugs, needlepoint rugs are stitched onto a canvas base, which is made up of even warp and weft threads. There are only three main types of canvas: single (or mono), double thread, and interlock (all available in white or a creamy 'antique' cotton). For making rugs, the polished 'mono de luxe' canvas, which is made up of heavier-gauge threads than ordinary mono canvas, is the strongest. However, as the largest mesh size available for this is usually 10 holes per inch, you may prefer to use a double canvas with 6/7 or 8/9 holes. Even larger-mesh rug canvas, with 3/4 holes, is also available for very thick yarns, or alternatively you can use Sudan canvas – a large-hole canvas specially produced for use with thicker yarns, which has meshes of 6 and 7 holes per inch.

Wool and silk have both been favoured for needlepoint since medieval times; today, however, wool is the principal yarn used. Not only is it the most hard-wearing of the natural fibres, but it has the added advantage of being very low in static electricity, which means that it doesn't attract dirt very easily. Several manufacturers produce both crewel and tapestry wools specifically for needle-point, in wide ranges of colours.

It's also possible to use knitting wools for this technique, although it's best to avoid the softer baby yarns and instead use the tougher Shetland-type quality. For making needlepoint rugs, though, any of the wools used for weaving are even more hard-wearing, because they are firmly twisted. Alternatively, other natural yarns such as linen, silk and cotton can be suitable, as can the stronger synthetic ones such as polyester and nylon. (For many years now manufac-turers of tufted carpets have added 20% nylon to their wool, to increase the carpet's wearing properties and resilience.)

Novelty yarns, such as metallic, bouclé and mohair, can also be included, although you may need to com-bine many strands to create a yarn thick enough to cover the canvas. You can also cut fabric strips to an appropriate width for the mesh size, and stitch them as if you were using yarn (see Fig 5.1).

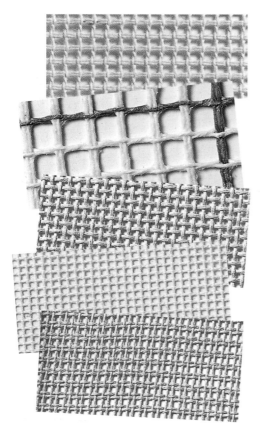

Needlepoint canvases, from the top: Sudan canvas, rug canvas, mono, interlock, double

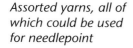

Assorted yarns, all of which could be used for needlepoint

A non-fraying, closely-woven fabric is best for this; fine knits also work well, and both of these can be used over wool or fabric to give a padded effect (Fig 5.2).

Each different combination of yarn, fabric and canvas will have different wearing properties, so bear this in mind when you're thinking about the rug's eventual use. These days, though, many rugs are placed in interiors to provide a decorative focus, so if you think your rug may be a little delicate you can always position it somewhere where it won't have daily wear. And, of course, there's always the option of hanging it on the wall.

Fig 5.1

Equipment and tools

When needlepoint is being used for small items, stitchers are divided over the advantages and disadvantages of using a frame. However, for needlepoint rugs, it's essential that the canvas is held at a consistent tension while it's being stitched, to avoid canvas distortion and an uneven stitched surface.

Even the largest hand frames – 69cm (27in) and 76cm (30in) wide – are impractical for rug making, since the work would become very heavy and cumbersome as the rug was stitched. With this kind of frame there's the added disadvantage that you can only view a 30cm (12in) length of the work at any one time, before winding it on. Floor frames are much stronger, especially the hardwood ones, and are available in greater widths of up to 178cm (70in).

You can, however, stitch a rug in smaller sections and then join the sections together. This is necessary in any case if you're stitching a very wide rug, as Zweigart canvases have a maximum width of 122cm (48in). If you do need to join sections of canvas for your design, it always looks best if you stitch a central panel and add borders, rather than making a join directly down the centre.

The only other pieces of equipment needed are a needle and sharp scissors. Select a tapestry needle that's the appropriate size for the yarns and the canvas that you're using. The eye of the needle should be large enough to enable the yarn to fit through it freely, but not be so large that the needle forces the canvas threads apart when you pull it through a hole in the canvas.

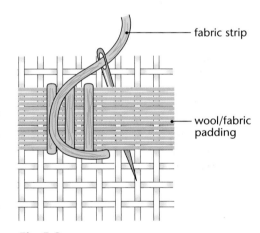

fabric strip

wool/fabric padding

Fig 5.2

Design considerations

♦ The most obvious design constraint for any needlepoint project is the regular grid created by the squares of the canvas. A very large mesh will produce a noticeable stepped effect around any curved shapes or lines, as well as making any detailed design almost impossible. You can easily overcome this problem by using a smaller-gauge canvas, but then the extra time required for the stitching may become an issue.

It's interesting to note how rapidly the number of stitches per square inch increases as the canvas gauge becomes smaller: for instance, if you're stitching on 6 holes per inch (hpi) canvas you'll work 36 stitches per square inch; on 10 hpi it will be 100, and on 16 hpi it will be 256! In recent years stitchers have been experimenting with different ways of producing a more free-flowing effect with canvaswork, including couching threads (see page 62) onto the surface of the canvas, weaving fabric strips and threads into the canvas, and the use of machine embroidery alongside the needlepoint.

♦ Decorative stitches will cover the canvas more quickly than the usual tent stitch, as well as providing valuable textural interest. This is well illustrated by the *Poppy Rug* (opposite), where the tent stitch contrasts well with the decorative trammed straight stitching.

♦ The *Poppy Rug* also demonstrates how well you can stitch very detailed pictorial elements in needlepoint (left), something which is impossible to achieve using any of the other rug techniques.

♦ The need to cover all the canvas could be viewed as another design constraint; this makes it difficult to work with free combinations of straight, diagonal and composite stitches because they cover the canvas to differing extents. However, in recent years it's become more common to leave some of the canvas bare, especially when it has been painted or coloured beforehand. Some stitchers also use overlays of sheer and semi-sheer fabrics, positioned before stitching, which partially obscure the canvas grid.

Working instructions

If you want to draw the design to be worked directly onto your canvas, do this with a permanent marker pen before attaching the canvas to the edges of the frame.

Cut the canvas to size, including an extra allowance of 5–8cm (2–3in) on each edge, then attach each edge of the canvas shape securely to the frame to ensure a strong and even tension across the work. Don't be tempted to hem the canvas edges before doing the stitching: this would make them far too thick to attach to the frame.

The following are general guidelines for stitching:

Fig 5.3

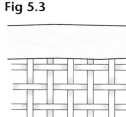

- ♦ Cover all the cut canvas edges with masking tape or bias binding to prevent any snagging of the yarn while you're stitching (Fig 5.3).
- ♦ Use lengths of yarn no longer than 50–70cm (20–30in) to prevent them tangling and wearing as you pull them through the canvas.
- ♦ At frequent intervals, let the needle and thread dangle freely to remove any excessive twisting.
- ♦ Start all yarns with a knot on the right side of the canvas, a short distance away from where you will be beginning to stitch. Once the thread on the wrong side has been secured with stitches (Fig 5.4), then cut away the knot.
- ♦ When you need to finish a thread, pass it through several stitches on the wrong side (Fig 5.5), then cut off the end.

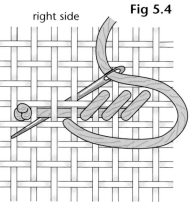

right side

Fig 5.4

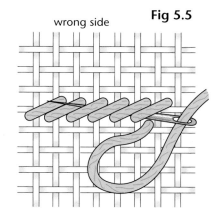

wrong side

Fig 5.5

Finishing

Stretching and blocking

Once the stitching is finished, remove the rug from the frame. If the corners are no longer square, the work will need stretching and blocking to straighten it. This can normally be carried out fairly easily at home, but the sheer size of the rug may make the process quite strenuous.

You will need the following equipment:

♦ a flat wooden board larger than the rug
♦ blotting paper larger than the rug (join several pieces with clear tape if necessary)
♦ drawing pins (thumbtacks) or tacks
♦ a hammer
♦ a water spray bottle (the kind that you use for spraying plants, or spraying on water when ironing).

Lightly dampen both sides of the canvas with a fine spray of water. Mark the finished size and shape of the rug onto the blotting paper, and lay the paper on the board. Pin the canvas out to the drawn shape on the blotting paper, pulling it in the appropriate directions as necessary (Fig 5.6). Leave the canvas to dry thoroughly, which may take a few days. If the rug is still distorted, or returns to its distorted shape after a few hours, repeat the process. A coat of thin wallpaper paste applied to the wrong side will help to it to retain the corrected shape.

If you don't like the idea of blocking the rug yourself, most needlework shops do offer a stretching service.

Fig 5.6

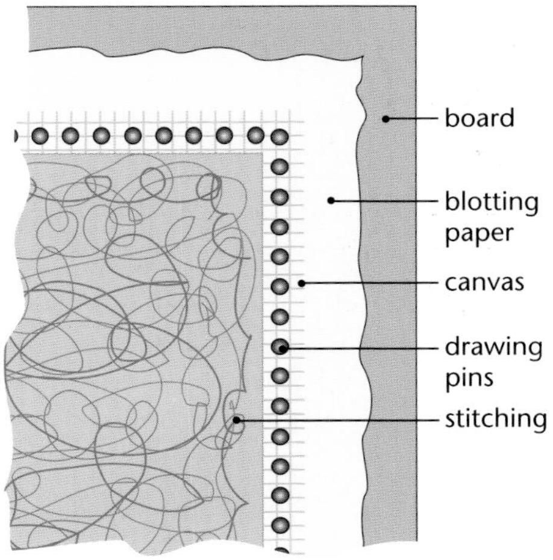

board
blotting paper
canvas
drawing pins
stitching

Joining sections

If the rug has been stitched in separate pieces, leave unstitched the final 1.25cm (½in) of the design on each of the edges to be joined. Block and stretch each of the pieces separately before joining them.

To join two pieces of canvas, fold back 2.5cm (1in) of the unstitched canvas on one side, and place over the edge of the other canvas section. Pin the pieces together, then tack them into position, matching up the two sides of the design exactly (Fig 5.7).

Fig 5.7

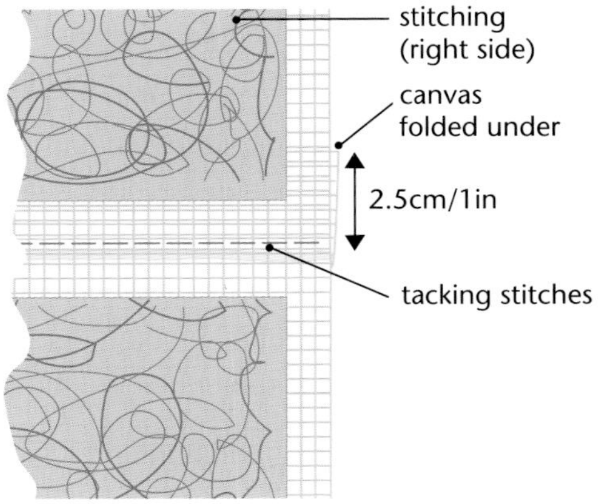

stitching (right side)
canvas folded under
2.5cm/1in
tacking stitches

Fig 5.8

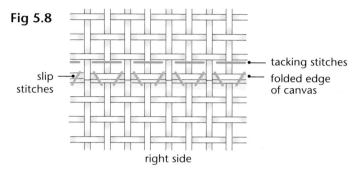

slip stitches

tacking stitches

folded edge of canvas

right side

Slip-stitch along the join using linen thread (Fig 5.8), then remove the tacking stitches. Continue the needlepoint stitching over the join, holding the extra unstitched canvas away from the back of the work, so that you're only stitching through a single thickness.

Neatening the edges

When all the stitching, joining (if necessary) and blocking is complete, turn the unworked canvas edges to the wrong side and stitch them with herringbone (Fig 5.9), using a linen thread.

Fig 5.9

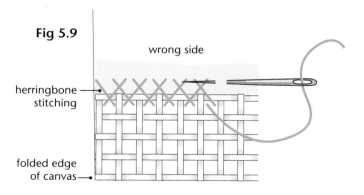

wrong side

herringbone stitching

folded edge of canvas

If there is any exposed canvas showing along the edges, then a row of matching needlepoint stitches can be worked to cover this (Fig 5.10), or the edges can be whipped (see page 63).

Cut a piece of curtain interlining or thin carpet felt very slightly smaller than the finished rug size, and lay it onto the wrong side of the canvas; stitch it into position with herringbone. Cut a piece of hessian roughly 10cm (4in) larger in each direction than the finished rug; turn each edge under by 5cm (2in) and press; lay the hessian over the interlining or felt, and secure it with a line of slip stitch (Fig 5.11).

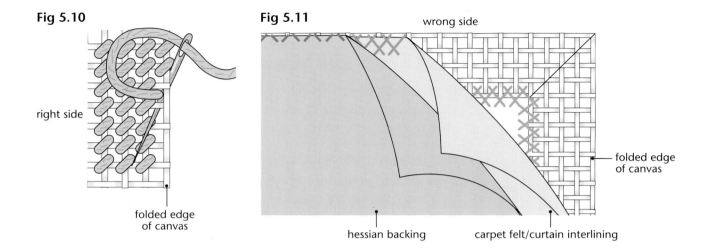

Fig 5.10

right side

folded edge
of canvas

Fig 5.11

wrong side

folded edge
of canvas

hessian backing

carpet felt/curtain interlining

Variations

There are hundreds of different needlepoint stitches, which can be roughly classified into straight, pile, knotted, composite, crossed and diagonal stitches. (Many different stitches are shown in my previous book, *Needlepoint: A Foundation Course*.) Even though many of these stitches have been in existence for hundreds of years, the endless combinations of stitch and yarn can still make the technique seem new and original. The *Poppy Rug* (see page 51) is a good example of mixing both diagonal and straight stitches.

There is also a vast array of yarns available to the stitcher: different colours, textures and materials. The possibilities created by the various combinations of stitches and yarn make needlepoint designing an exciting challenge. You can take the technique further, too, by combining it with another rug-making technique such as hooking, prodding, locker- or latch-hooking, creating innovative and highly original pieces of work.

NEEDLEPOINT PROJECT
Blue and Purple Rug

MATERIALS

- 7hpi Zweigart canvas in cream, 79 x 66cm (31 x 26in)
- 2.5m (2½yd) medium piping cord
- Ten hanks DMC tapestry wool in white
- Eight skeins DMC tapestry wool in royal blue
- Eight 12m (roughly 12yd) skeins of two-ply silk, undyed
- One 220g (roughly 8oz) skein of mercerized two-ply cotton, undyed
- One 450g (1lb) skein of six-ply linen, white
- One 100g (roughly 3½oz) cone of double knitting viscose ribbon, white
- Omega all-in-one acid dyes, in blue, purple and aqua
- Tapestry needle, size 20

This is a very decorative rug, made using mixed yarns and a variety of stitches, worked in bands of randomly arranged patterns. The threads I've used include tapestry wool, silk, linen and cotton yarns, together with a small amount of knitting ribbon. All of these have been dyed with varying concentrations of blue, aqua and purple dyes – although you could use plain or ready-dyed threads if you prefer. Just choose yarns in your preferred colours instead of white, and skip the dyeing part of the instructions. I've edged each section of the pattern with a couched cord, and finished the rug with a knotted fringe made from the leftover lengths of thread.

FINISHED SIZE: 68 x 55cm (27 x 22in), including the fringe

Working instructions

DYEING

The first task is to dye your fabrics. Wind approximately 10m (10yd) lengths from the large cones and skeins, and place several ties around each hank to hold it together, then wet each yarn hank and squeeze it out. Follow the manufacturers' instructions for making up the blue dye, then immerse some of the undyed wool hanks into the dye solution. Sprinkle a few grains of the purple and aqua powders onto the wet wool, to create the space-dyed effect.

To obtain hanks of wool in lighter shades, drain away some of the dye liquid, and dilute the remainder by adding more hot water. Immerse the next batch of wool, and repeat the sprinkling of the additional colours. Finally, repeat the process a third time using very little dye, so that these hanks are quite pale.

The silk, cotton, linen and ribbon are mostly dyed in solid colours, using varying strengths of the three dye colours to achieve different shades. (A small quantity of each of these yarns can also be space-dyed with the wool, to give you more variation in stitching.)

PREPARATION AND STITCHING

The only part of the design that needs to be transferred to the canvas is the pattern of vertical lines (Fig 5.12). Using the given measurements, which are only approximate guides, draw wiggly lines on the canvas with a permanent marker pen.

Fig 5.12

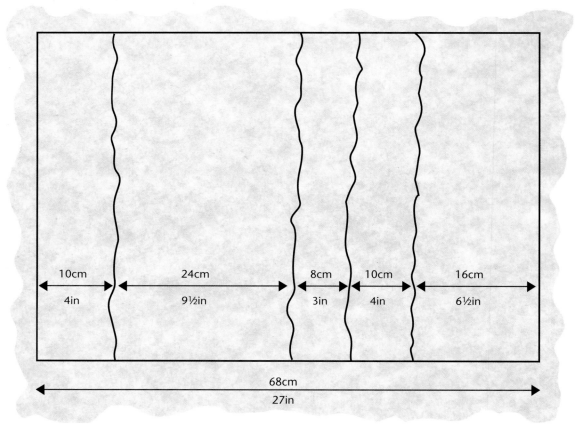

10cm
4in

24cm
9½in

8cm
3in

10cm
4in

16cm
6½in

68cm
27in

Then, cover the entire rug with lines of tramming in blue tapestry wool. (This is an excellent opportunity to use up oddments left over from previous projects.) The tramming threads partially cover the canvas mesh, so that it will be less visible when you're working some of the decorative stitches and using the finer yarns.

Create tramming lines by working long straight stitches across the canvas as shown (Fig 5.13); stagger the ends of the lines so that they don't create a bump or dip in the stitched surface.

Each patterned panel is built up using different random combinations of the following stitches: straight, wheatsheaf, Florentine, French knots and bullion knots.

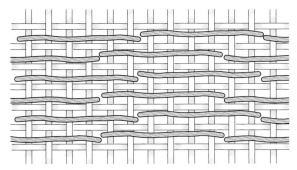

Fig 5.13

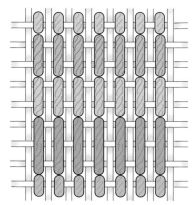

Fig 5.14

Straight stitch

Straight stitches are worked over one, two or three canvas threads, using two strands of tapestry wool (Fig 5.14). Each panel starts and finishes with several rows of these straight stitches, and then they recur at irregular intervals throughout each panel.

Wheatsheaf stitch

Wheatsheaf stitch is formed from three straight stitches, worked over four, six, eight or ten canvas threads, held together with a horizontal stitch across the centre (Fig 5.15). I've worked complete rows of the stitch in varying sizes (Fig 5.16), as well as rows interspersed with small straight stitches (Fig 5.17). The wool, silk, linen and cotton yarns have been used for this stitch, in each case using two strands of yarn in the needle at once.

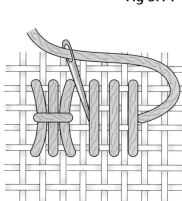

Fig 5.15

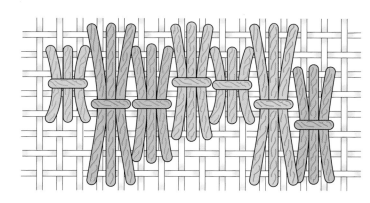

Fig 5.16

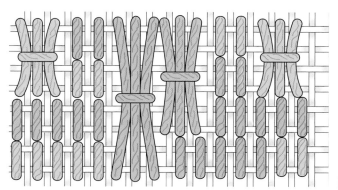

Fig 5.17

Florentine stitch

This stitch is created by working straight stitches over one, two, three, four and five threads of the canvas in stepped patterns, with small areas of French knots in between (Fig 5.18). Again, I've used a mixture of threads, including the ribbon, to create the Florentine stitches.

Fig 5.18

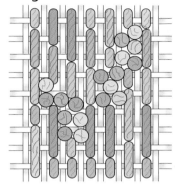

French knots

As well as including French knots alongside the areas worked with Florentine stitch, I've also worked them, either on their own or in conjunction with bullion knots (Fig 5.19), at the ends or in the middle of very long straight stitches. I've worked the knots in all the various yarns, using one or two threads depending on the size of knot required. Make each French knot by bringing the needle to the front of the canvas and winding the thread round it two or three times (Fig 5.20a); then pull the twists tight (b) and take the needle back down through the same hole.

Fig 5.19

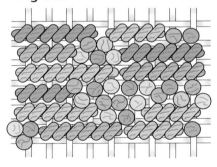

Fig 5.20a

b

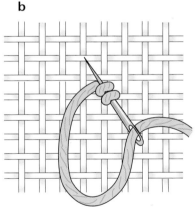

Bullion knots

I've also used all the various threads to stitch the bullion knots (Fig 5.21a, b and c), working them alongside the French knots, and again using either one or two strands as appropriate.

To begin each bullion knot, bring the needle to the front of the work. Take it down again several threads away, bringing the tip up again where the thread emerges, and wind the thread around the needle several times (Fig 5.21a). Pull the needle and thread through the twists so that they form a long, tight twisted stitch (b), then take the needle back down through the canvas so that the bullion knot lies in a flat line along the canvas (c).

Fig 5.21a

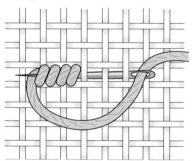

b

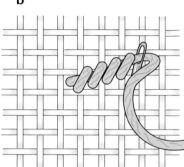

c

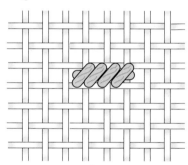

Work each complete panel of patterns before you begin the next, and leave a gap of two canvas threads unstitched along each of the marked lines; these create gaps for the piping cord to be couched into place.

Couching

When all the needlepoint is finished, lay a length of piping cord along each marked line and thread your needle with two strands of the blue tapestry wool; work straight stitches across the cord, stitching into every hole so that the cord is completely covered (Fig 5.22).

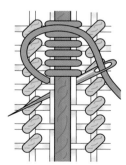

Fig 5.22

FINISHING

Along the top edge of the rug, fold the unstitched canvas to the wrong side, as close as possible to the last row of stitching, and secure with herringbone stitch (see page 54). Along the bottom edge, fold the excess canvas to the wrong side but leave one row of unstitched canvas showing; the fringe will be attached to this. At each side, leave two threads of unstitched canvas showing; when you have secured the excess at the back, whip these using two threads of tapestry wool (Fig 5.23).

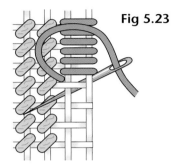

Fig 5.23

The fringe is created by working overhand knots (see page 136), using single strands of all the threads used to stitch the rug. Leave a small space at each side and underneath each couched line, so that you can attach small tassels made from the silk yarn (see page 140). Trim the fringe and tassels to approximately 5cm (2in).

Prodded Rugs

THERE ARE MANY regional names for prodded rugs; 'proddy', 'clippy', 'tabbie', 'pooked', 'proggy' and 'broggy' are just some of them. Unlike needlepoint rugs, which have always been an occupation for the leisured classes who had money to spend on wools and silks, prodded rugs have very humble origins among the working classes. This kind of rug was particularly popular in the north of England and in Wales during the late nineteenth century and through to the Second World War; prodded rugs could be produced at virtually no cost, making use of old hessian or burlap feed and sugar sacks together with worn-out clothing.

In recent years there has been a renewal of interest in prodded rugs, along with many other crafts – heightened in this case by environmental concerns and a keenness for recycling. Compared with the materials available to the early makers of prodded rugs, today there is a far wider variety of fabrics which can easily be acquired and used. The textural and visual effects of Lurex and Lycra (Spandex), fleece, flock and sweatshirt fabrics, denim, carrier bags and foil packaging can be quite exciting when prodded. Current rag rug workers such as Ben Hall, Ali Rhind and Julia Burrows are producing prodded pieces which are both innovative and creative.

Fig 6.1

Fig 6.2

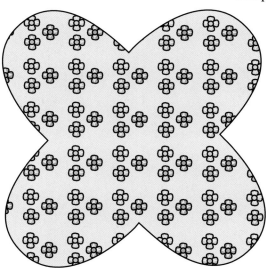

Materials

Prodded rugs are created by pushing strips of fabric through an open-weave base material – traditionally hessian or burlap. The 12oz hessian is preferable to the cheaper and thinner 10oz, which has thinner threads that can sometimes break. The American cotton monk's cloth is my preferred base material, although you can use any fabric which is strong, doesn't stretch and has a fairly open weave of evenly balanced warp and weft threads: for instance linen, cotton or a synthetic mesh fabric.

The earliest prodded mats were made out of old clothes, and therefore tended largely to use strips of cotton, which flattened quickly. For a rug that is to be well used today, wool is preferable because of its resilient qualities; you can obtain woollen strips by cutting up old garments and blankets. New wool flannel is sold specifically for rag rug making, and is available either in white, ready to dye, or in a range of colours. However, depending on the use of the rug, any fabric which has a reasonably tight weave or close knit, and doesn't fray excessively, could be used, for instance synthetics, towelling, denim (Fig 6.1), velour, satin, plastic, leather and suede. For purely decorative work, materials such as paper, crisp packets and netting can create intriguing effects. If you're considering making a prodded rug, it's a useful exercise to create samples trying out some of these different fabrics; include various patterned ones, too, such as checks (see page 65), tweed, florals (Fig 6.2, made using pieces of fabric cut in the flower shape shown), and geometrics.

The quantity of fabric needed for a rug of a particular size depends, of course, on the thickness and length of the fabric strips, as well as the density of the prodding. Once again, you'll find it invaluable to make a sample before you start the rug, to give you a rough idea of the number and length of strips you'll require. As a very approximate guide, a given area of base fabric will need four times its length and twice its width in fabric to be cut up into strips.

Equipment and tools

The main piece of equipment you'll require is a prodder, a small hand tool with a smooth, pointed metal end, for pushing or prodding the fabric strips through the base material. A frame is optional; it's both quicker and easier to prod the hessian if it's held taut, but some rug workers still prefer the flexibility of holding the base fabric by hand. If you do choose to work on a frame, you can use an adjustable floor frame, stitching the hessian to the top and bottom tapes, or an artist's canvas stretcher (which can be supported by trestles or chairs), where the hessian is attached with staples or drawing pins.

Strip-cutting machines, which cut fabrics accurately into a choice of different widths, speed up the process of strip preparation considerably. Alternatively, a rotary cutter and mat can be quicker than the more traditional scissors. Whichever method you choose, the fabric should be cut along the warp threads, or down the length of knitted fabrics, in order to keep fraying to a minimum.

The width of the strips will vary according to the fabric that you're using, but as a general guide cut thin to medium fabrics into 1cm (⅜in) widths, and medium to thick fabrics into 2.5cm (1in) widths. The length of the strips is directly related to how shaggy you want the pile of the rug to be, but again as a general rule 10cm (4in) is about the maximum workable length for a long pile, with a minimum of 6cm (2½in) for a closer-cut pile.

Design considerations

♦ In contrast to needlepoint rugs, prodded ones are unable to produce very much design detail because of their deep shaggy surface and the coarseness of the mesh they are worked on. Any design lines become blurred when prodded, and may be lost completely if they are too fine, so use simple, bold designs.

♦ Prodded rugs have been likened to the pointillist style of paintings, which rely on a mass of coloured dots to convey an image; often a prodded design is only properly visible if the rug is some distance away. Many designers of prodded rugs rely on the mix of different types and colours of fabric to create a variegated or striped effect.

Working instructions

As hessian frays badly, it's best to hem it before you begin the prodding. Turn the raw edges to the back and secure them either by machine stitching or slip stitching. When you're working on the edges of the design, prod the fabric strips through both layers of the hessian.

Draw or transfer your design to the wrong side of the base material, as this is the side from which you'll be doing the prodding. Then select your fabrics and cut them into strips. Decide which part of the design you are going to work first (it's always best to work individual motifs before you work the background), then use the prodder to make a hole for the first strip of fabric. Push the strip half-way through the hole (Fig 6.3a), then make a second hole with the prodder approximately 2–4 hessian threads away from the first. Push the other end of the strip through this hole to the right side of the fabric (b) and pull it tight, so that the ends of the fabric strip are even (c).

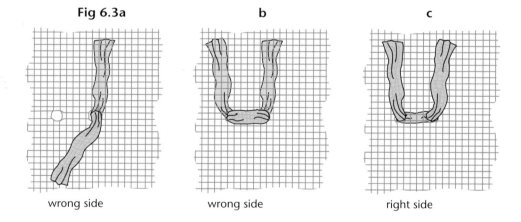

Fig 6.3a   b   c

wrong side   wrong side   right side

When you begin the next strip, you can either start by pushing it through the final hole used for the first strip, or create a new starting hole a few threads away, depending on the thickness of the fabric you're using. Once all the prodding is completed, trim any uneven ends with scissors.

Finishing

Latex adhesive is often recommended for use on prodded rugs as a bonding agent; it's applied to the back when the rug is completed. This not only strengthens the hessian and provides a non-slip surface, but also ensures that there's no risk of any of the prodded fabric pieces moving or working themselves back down through the base holes. A backing fabric is optional, but does tend to make the rug more durable as well as making the back neater. You can glue the backing in place with more latex, or slip-stitch it as for needlepoint rugs (see page 55).

Variations

Fig 6.4

If you want to create a more linear effect with your prodded strips, try using rug canvas as the base fabric instead of hessian. A good example of this is the Lurex prodded sample (Fig 6.4), worked on 3.5hpi canvas.

If you'd like to try a slightly more detailed design using the prodding technique, you can substitute thick wools for the fabric pieces; you'll find that you need to place them very close together in order to cover the base material fully.

Working some areas in prodding and some in uncut hooking (see page 76) creates an attractive contrast in textures.

Piping or braided bands form decorative edges for prodded rugs.

'Hit or miss' patterns, i.e. completely random designs, were popular with the early American colonists, and can be achieved by using up any odd bits and pieces of fabric and yarn. If you prefer a slightly less haphazard version of this approach, overdye your fabrics and yarns beforehand (see page 20).

Experiment with using different fabric shapes for prodding rather than the long rectangular strip. This technique has been pioneered by an American rug hooker, Gloria Crouse; she has successfully used squares and circles, with pinked or plain-cut edges, poked through a single hole in the base fabric (Fig 6.5a) and secured with a dab of glue on the wrong side (b). See also the flower shapes on page 66.

Fig 6.5a   **b**

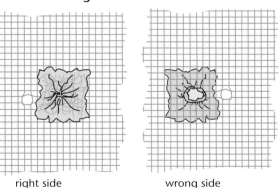

right side   wrong side

Hooked Rugs

HOOKED RUGS have always been the most common and also the most versatile of all the rag rug techniques, both in Britain, which has a long history of rug hooking, and in America, where the technique was introduced in the 1840s by settlers from Britain. Rug hooking has become virtually a way of life in many parts of America, not only as a thriving hobby and small industry, but as an art form, with numerous examples to be found in art galleries as well as museums.

As with prodded rugs (see page 64), this technique flourished in Britain in the poor and rural areas, particularly the north of England where there was a ready supply of fabrics and yarns from the mills. It was only around the middle of the twentieth century that people tended to discard this thrifty technique. Since that time there has been a slow and gradual revival of interest, fuelled by well-known artists such as Winifred Nicholson, who set up rug hooking classes in the 1960s. Today, colleges all over Britain offer hooking courses, and rug workers such as Lizzy Reakes, Lynne Stein, Jufu Vail and Liz Kitching are producing both inspiring and original work which is a long way from the hooked rugs of the nineteenth century.

These modern artists often mix rug making techniques, and use both recycled and new fabrics, together with yarns, plastics, foils, silks, metallics and novelty threads in vibrant colours, in their imaginative contemporary designs. There are now many designers who, as well as working on commissioned pieces, produce kits for making hooked rugs, and the Association of Rag Rug Makers, based in London, is going from strength to strength.

Fig 7.1

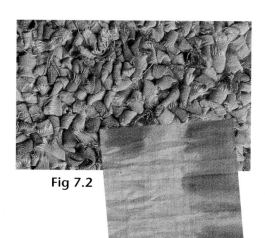

Fig 7.2

Materials and yarns

The base fabrics for hooked rugs are essentially the same as for prodded ones (see page 66). It's now possible to buy a sturdier version of the cotton monk's cloth, an American fabric also known as warp cloth; it has the distinct advantage of stretching less than some of the other base fabrics, which has made it a popular choice.

It's possible to hook either yarn or strips of fabric through the background to create the characteristic loops; many rug makers favour yarn, as it's possible to create finer details and also there is no problem of fraying edges. Fabrics, though, offer many other possible effects – and of course you can mix the two in the same piece. Today's rug hookers exploit the different characteristics of the huge variety of fabrics and yarns available, often achieving unusual and exciting textures (Fig 7.1).

'Fuzzy' yarns or fabrics such as mohair, angora, chenille and velvet, all of which make soft loops, can be contrasted with well-defined loops of smoother materials such as cotton, linen and plastic. You can introduce metallics – either yarns or fabrics – as highlights; shiny fabrics such as satin, moiré, silk and PVC can be used in the same way. Upholstery fabrics, for instance damask, brocade, brocatelle, moquette, Dralon, tweed and ottoman, shouldn't be overlooked. Of course you can also use dyed fabrics and yarns to produce variegated and patterned surfaces, as well as for producing co-ordinated colour ranges (Fig 7.2).

Before you begin a hooked rug, it's useful to estimate the amount of each fabric or yarn you'll need to hook each of the different parts of the design. As an approximate guide, if you're using fabric allow four times the area being hooked. For yarn, allow 2kg per square metre or 4lb per square yard. It's always a good idea to produce a sample using your chosen fabric or yarn on your chosen base fabric; this will give you a more accurate guide, which is especially valuable if only a limited quantity of a particular fabric is available. If one specific fabric is in short supply, an easy solution is to mix it with another fabric of a similar colour. This will produce a slightly mottled surface, which will certainly be more interesting than a solid colour.

Equipment and tools

Your first requirement is a rug hook (below). A rug hook has a handle (usually made of wood), and a metal spike with a fairly sharp hooked point. These hooks vary in width from very fine (no. 1) to a much heavier version (no. 10). These days rug hooks are widely available, and are a great improvement on the early versions – created from a nail bent to form a hook by the local blacksmith, and inserted into a piece of wood.

As for prodded rugs, a frame is optional and is a matter of personal choice, although having the base fabric held under tension does seem to improve the evenness of the hooking. In America, where rug hooking is very popular, there is a vast array of frames to choose from, including a fold-up version of a lap frame specifically designed for taking on your travels. If you do decide to use a frame, it's a good idea not only to machine-stitch the edges of the hessian base first to prevent them from fraying, but to attach strips of herringbone tape as well. These strips then provide a strong edge which can be laced to the frame. Before you machine the edges, find the straight grain of the hessian on each edge by pulling out a thread (Fig 7.3).

Napping scissors (see page 76) have bent handles, and are essential if you want to shear your loops or sculpt the pile into a particular shape. Machines which cut strips of fabric, known as cloth strippers or slitters, obviously speed up the process enormously, especially as several layers of fabric can be cut at one time. However, some of these will only operate on natural fabrics, as synthetics blunt the blades. Most machines will cut strips into widths of 2mm (¹⁄₁₆in), up to a maximum of 12.5mm (½in). This facility for cutting very narrow strips easily and accurately has made more detailed and intricate rug designs possible. If you want to use fabrics that fray for hooking, cut the strips wider than usual so that they can be folded in half down their length and used double.

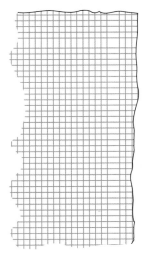

Fig 7.3

Fig 7.4

Fig 7.5

Design considerations

♦ In contrast to the rather vague design possibilities of prodded rugs, hooked ones offer vast scope for creativity and pictorial detail. Obviously this depends on the type and thickness of fabric strips or yarns that you are hooking, but fine yarns on a canvas base can produce as much detail as a needlepoint rug.

♦ Designs aren't only limited to pictorial designs and varying colours, but can involve textural interest as well. This can be created in many ways, not only by the mix of fabrics and yarns, but also by placing thick strips with fine strips, by working contour hooking (see page 76), and by using a combination of sheared and unsheared loops.

♦ There are many ways of creating surfaces which are variegated in colour and tone. Try blending similar shades of the same type of fabric, or different fabrics of the same colour (Fig 7.4). Using patterned fabrics such as tweeds will produce an all-over variegation; small patterned fabrics often produce a spotty effect when they are hooked (Fig 7.5, with the loops shown cut and uncut). Try hooking two fabrics together at the same time, so that when these are sheared, both the colours will show on the surface (Fig 7.6). You can also dye your fabrics before hooking to create non-solid colours (see pages 18–21).

Fig 7.6

Working instructions

Transfer the design to the base fabric; this can be done by using tracing or carbon paper, by drawing round a series of templates, or by copying your design freehand onto the base fabric. Once you've completed the transfer, reinforce any faint lines with a permanent marker, then you're ready to start the hooking.

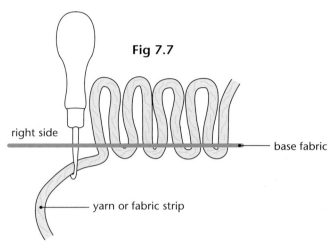

Fig 7.7

right side

base fabric

yarn or fabric strip

Hook all the outlines first, then fill in any individual shapes and motifs, leaving the background until last. Start by holding a long strip of fabric or yarn beneath the base fabric; push the hook through the fabric from the right side, hook the tip around the fabric or yarn, and pull it up to form a loop (Fig 7.7).

Repeat this process, leaving roughly 2–4 threads of the base fabric between the loops, depending on the thickness of the strips. (Try out a sample first to practise the height and width of the loops. If they are hooked too close to each other, the hessian will stretch and buckle; if they are too widely spaced, the hessian will be visible between them.)

On average your finished loops, if you're using fabric strips, should be as tall as they are wide, although if you're going to shear the loops you should make them slightly taller. Once you've finished hooking each length of yarn or strip of fabric, bring the raw ends up to the right side to prevent unravelling. At each edge of the rug, it's best to work the loops very close together for the outer 5cm (2in) to form a firm, hard-wearing edge.

Hooking is usually worked around shapes or lines in the design, rather than in straight lines. This is called contour hooking, and it tends to accentuate and give more definition to a design (Fig 7.8). It's also a good method for making a large background more interesting; you can introduce random shapes across the background, then echo them with lines of hooking (Fig 7.9).

Fig 7.8   **Fig 7.9**

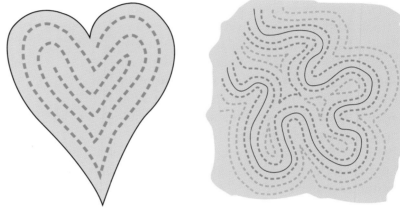

Finishing

The loops can either be left as they are, or sheared to give a neater, denser look to the hooking.

If the rug looks creased or flattened when the hooking is finished, steam it (with the steam iron held a short distance away from the surface) to revitalize it. To neaten the edges, turn the raw edges to the wrong side and secure them with herringbone stitch, then add binding tape to create a firm, hard-wearing edge.

Napping scissors, or carpet shears, which can be used for cutting the loops of your hooked rug

This tape should be slip-stitched in position; if you want to add a lining or backing fabric to the rug, position it over the wrong side of the rug and add the binding tape over both layers (Fig 7.10).

Alternatively, you can create a decorative edge which will be visible from the right side. Use herringbone tape in a matching colour, or add a binding made from some other fabric. The *Fruit Rug* (see page 80) has its edges finished in this way; I made the binding out of strips left over from the hooking, joining the different coloured strips randomly.

Variations

Any of the techniques that rely on the same kind of base fabric can be mixed with hooking on the same project – for example, hooking and prodding (page 64), or hooking and punch needling (page 78).

If you work hooking on canvas instead of hessian, then it can be mixed with needlepoint (page 46), locker and latch hooking (pages 86 and 96) and rya knotting (page 131).

It's also possible to work hooking in conjunction with appliquéd shapes; stitch these to the base fabric first, then work the hooking around them. Braiding plus hooking is a favourite combination, especially using the braiding as an attractive border or edging.

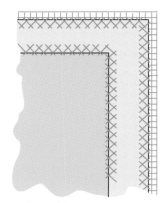

Fig 7.10

Other methods of hooking

Three other types of hook are used for making simple hooked rugs. These are: the punch needle, the speed or shuttle hook, and the *tappenalen* or eggbeater. All of these are twentieth-century products, and so fairly modern compared with the traditional hand hook; they were extremely popular in the 1920s and 30s. Each one has been designed to speed up the basic hooking process, as well as to achieve a more even and consistent surface.

The base fabric used for these other hooks is the same as for hand hooking, but it must be secured firmly to a frame; for the speed hook and *tappenalen*, the frame must be free-standing, so that the hessian can be pierced freely and both hands are available to hold the tools. Because you're using a frame it's advisable to reinforce the edges of the base fabric with tape.

Punch needle

Work from the wrong side of the base fabric. Thread the yarn through the needle; with the slotted side facing the direction in which you're working, push the needle through the fabric to push the raw end through to the front. Pull the needle through to the back again; hold it in a vertical position, lift it over two or three threads to the next loop position, and plunge the needle through the fabric again as far as it will go (Fig 7.11). Continue in the same way, making sure that all the ends finish on the right side of the work and are trimmed level with the loops. The yarn must be allowed to feed freely, or you will find yourself creating very short loops – or even no loops at all!

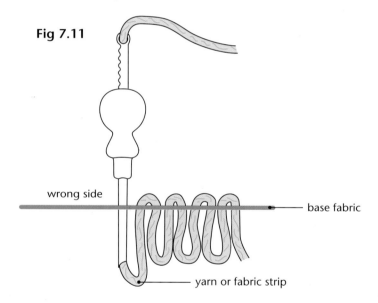

Fig 7.11

wrong side

base fabric

yarn or fabric strip

As well as producing loops more quickly than conventional hooking, the punch needle (when it's used correctly) automatically creates loops of an even length, between 5mm and 1cm (³⁄₁₆–³⁄₈in). The punch needle was originally designed for use with yarns, ribbons and braids, not fabrics, but as long as the fabric strips are cut narrow and even, and the fabric itself isn't too heavy, they will slide freely through the needle. The obvious disadvantage of the tool is that it can't be used for heavy, bulky fabrics, or even for some of the thicker, bulkier yarns.

Speed or shuttle hook

This hook is made from metal and wood, and shoots the yarn or fabric strips into the base fabric to form loops.

Work from the back of the fabric. Thread a length of yarn or strip of fabric through the eye of the needle and then through the loop at the side. Push the right section down so that the needle goes into the base fabric (Fig 7.12); as this is manually raised, the left section automatically lowers to secure the loop. The shuttle then automatically moves to the next position.

This tool is much quicker to use than the punch needle; it also accommodates all types of fabric and yarn, works in many directions and is easily adjustable to create loops of different heights. Its main disadvantage, as for all techniques worked from the wrong side, is that it's slightly less easy to follow a detailed design and to see how it's coming along as you work.

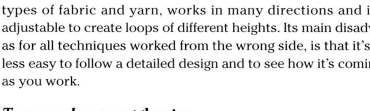

Fig 7.12

wrong side

base fabric

yarn or fabric strip

Tappenalen or eggbeater

This is a Danish hooking tool that moves automatically, making up to 500 loops per minute; its English name arose because, with its side-mounted handle, it looks rather like an old-fashioned eggwhisk. It has adjustable loop heights – 5mm–2.5cm (³⁄₁₆–1in), but it is difficult and time-consuming to thread. However, its main disadvantage is that it's manufactured for use with four-ply yarn (or the equivalent thickness) only. A strong cotton or linen base fabric is preferable to hessian for this aggressive tool.

HOOKED PROJECT
Fruit Rug

MATERIALS

- 10oz hessian, approximately 92 x 147cm (36 x 56in)
- dyed blankets cut into 7.5mm–1cm (roughly ⅜in) strips, in navy blue, maroon, dark pink, pink, red, orange, apricot, yellow, lemon, lime green, turquoise and blue. As a rough guide to the various amounts of fabric colours needed:
  – 25 x 50cm (10 x 20in) of pink, maroon, apricot and lemon
  – 50cm (20in) square of orange and yellow
  – 50cm x 1m (20 x 40in) of dark pink, lime green, red and navy blue
  – 1m (40in) square of turquoise
- a rug hook, medium size
- shears
- binding made from excess fabric, 4m (4yd) in total
- piece of 12oz hessian for the backing, approximately 77 x 132cm (30 x 52in)

Various fruits are featured on this rug, designed in six panels with patterned edgings, and surrounded by a decorative border. The hooking method lends itself well to areas and lines of one colour, rather than individual stitches. The entire rug has been made by hooking old, dyed blankets, which you can often obtain readily from charity shops or jumble sales; alternatively, use old woollen clothes, preferably felted, in the appropriate colours (or suitably dyed).

After I'd completed the hooking I sheared all the loops, which gives emphasis to the design details as well as creating a closer, tidier pile. I finished the edges with a decorative striped binding, made from the remaining pieces of dyed blanket.

FINISHED SIZE: approximately 72 x 127cm (28 x 50in)

Working instructions

DYEING

If you're dyeing the fabric, particularly for the blue and turquoise backgrounds, use one of the dyeing methods mentioned on pages 18–21 to create shading or variegations of colour; low-volume immersion and dip-dyeing work well. When this fabric is hooked, you'll find that it produces a much more interesting surface. For dip-dyeing with acid dyes, it's easier to begin with a dye solution in a strong colour; immerse part of the fabric, simmering as required, then remove the fabric and dilute the dye. Place more of the fabric in, simmer, then remove and dilute again; dip in the remaining fabric and simmer again to complete the dyeing.

TRANSFERRING THE DESIGN

As soon as you've cut the 10oz hessian to the correct size for the rug, zigzag the edges by machine to prevent any fraying while you're hooking (of course if any of the hessian edges are selvages, they don't need stitching).

Draw in the finished rug size on the hessian, then divide it into a grid of 18cm (7in) squares as shown (Fig 7.13). Now copy the design details freehand, using a black permanent marker pen. (As the 'not quite square' squares, and the irregular sizes and shapes of the fruit, are part of the charm of this rug design, it's not important to be accurate when you're creating your drawing.)

HOOKING

Using a cutting machine, a rotary cutter or scissors, cut the fabric into 1cm (⅜in) strips. Start the hooking with the outside edge lines, ensuring that you work this row along a straight line of the hessian. The loops on this rug should be 1.5cm (⅝in) tall, instead of the more usual 1cm (⅜in), as you'll be shearing them later. Next, hook the inner border lines – those around the six squares – and the outlines of any shapes within these.

Now start hooking the fruit shapes in the middle two panels. The diagrams (page 84) show the shading and the colours of the fabrics required. Each fruit is hooked in a rough spiral following the outline, working in from the edge and finishing in the centre, to help to create a three-dimensional effect.

Gradually work towards the edges of the rug, always hooking any motifs before backgrounds. The rug will become bulky and heavy as work progresses, and it's much easier to be left with outer areas to work rather than central ones. The background areas immediately around the fruit are also hooked by echoing the outlines; this emphasizes the shapes, as well as creating a more interesting surface. Leave about 4in (10cm) unhooked at each edge of the rug.

FINISHING

Use the shears to cut the loops to an even height. This is time-consuming, as well as hard on the hands, so I recommend that you shear one section at a time with a break in between to do something else and rest your hands.

Fold under 2.5cm (1in) turnings on the piece of 12oz backing hessian, and slip-stitch this fabric to the back of the rug.

Fig 7.13

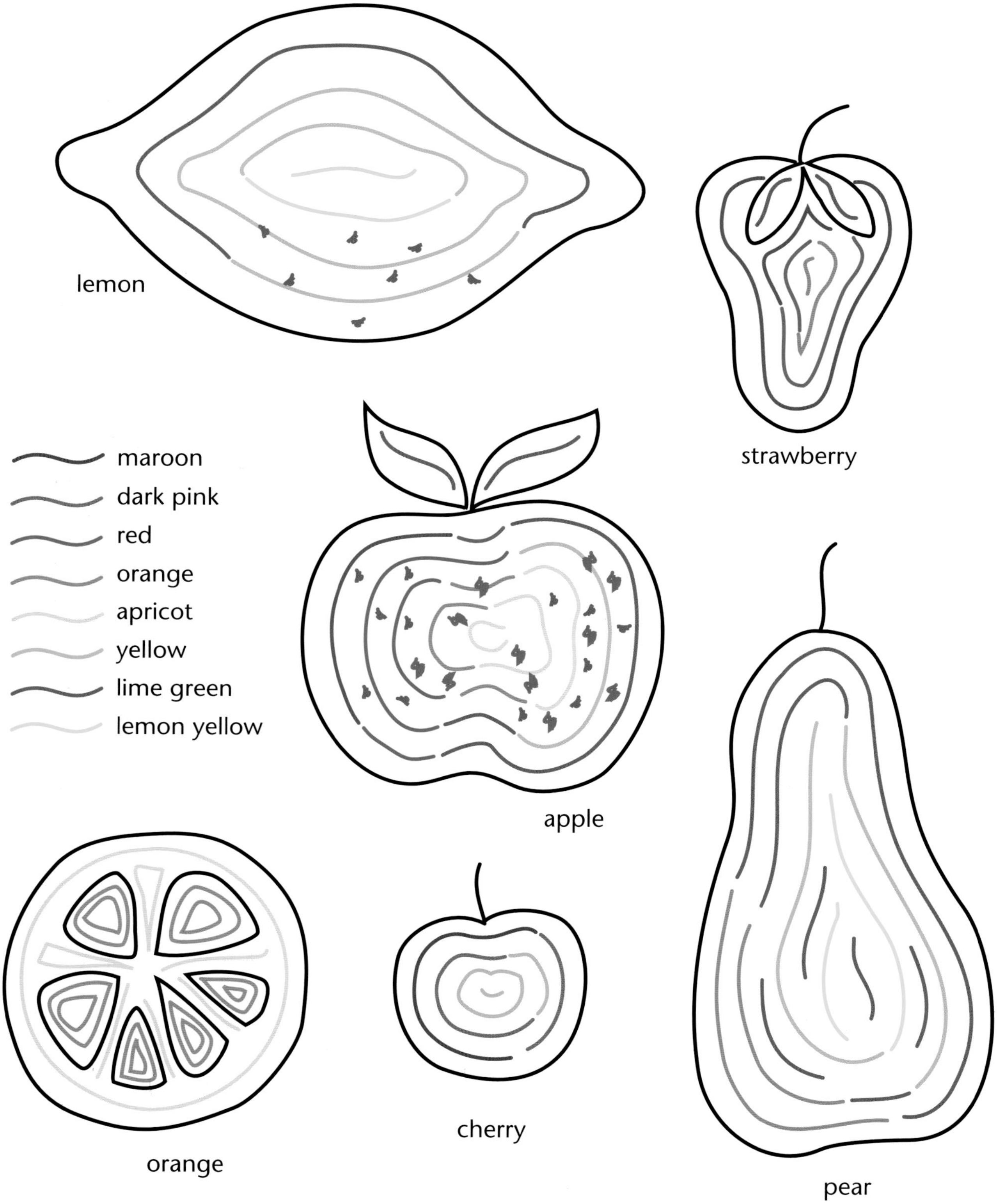

lemon

strawberry

maroon

dark pink

red

orange

apricot

yellow

lime green

lemon yellow

apple

orange

cherry

pear

To make the decorative binding, choose leftover pieces of blanket in different colours and cut them into 5cm (2in) wide strips, cutting on the diagonal grain of the fabric. Join the strips in an attractive sequence using cross-way seams (see page 31). With right sides together, tack this binding close to the first row of hooking all round the rug (Fig 7.14a), then machine-stitch. Join the two ends as shown (b and c).

Trim the 10oz hessian to 1.5cm (⅝in) beyond the machining and fold the binding over to the wrong side of the rug to cover the edge of the backing fabric; fold under the raw edges, and slip-stitch very close to the folded edge of the backing fabric.

Fig 7.14a   **b**   **c**

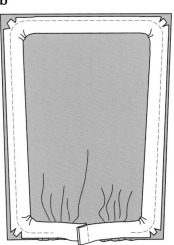

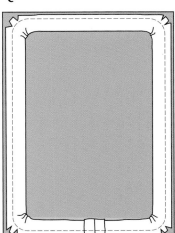

This detail of the rug shows the pieced binding

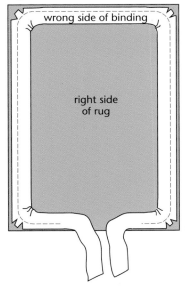

Locker-Hooked Rugs

LOCKER HOOKING is a twentieth-century invention, although it's difficult to date the innovation precisely. In both America and Australia it's possible to find rug makers using locker hooking, although the Americans call the method 'anchored loop', which is a good description. In fact, it's probable that this method was developed specifically to solve the problem of loops pulling out, on hooked and punched rugs, by anchoring them on the back.

Few books have been published on this method, although it's often briefly mentioned in books on other rug techniques. Its comparative lack of appeal may be because locker hooking is more limited in design possibilities and versatility than most of the other hand rug-making methods.

Materials and threads

Locker hooking requires mono or interlock tapestry canvas as the base fabric; the mesh size depends on the thickness of the fabric or yarn being used, and the finished texture you require. For a fairly chunky rug, such as the completed *Rainbow-Striped Mat* (see page 92), use a rug canvas with three to four holes per inch; for a closer weave, choose a six or seven-count mesh. If you're working on smaller items, such as cushions or bags, increase the mesh count of the base canvas size accordingly. You can use hessian, but this makes it more difficult to achieve a regular stitch texture.

Two threads are required for this technique: the first is used as the locking thread, for anchoring the loops, and the second is the fabric or yarn used for the loops themselves. Any fabric or yarn can be used for the loops, but it must be an appropriate thickness for the size of canvas. In Australia, long-staple fleece seems to be the predominant material used – uncombed, combed, carded, dyed (see top sample on page 87) or natural.

The choice of locking thread for a particular project depends partly on the material you're using for the loops, but it must be a strong thread, and preferably of a similar colour to the loop material unless you're deliberately trying to create a contrast. If you use the same thread for both purposes – looping and locking – it will produce a firm-textured surface; if you use a locking thread that is thinner than your loop material, the loops are not pulled so tightly around the thread, which produces a softer texture.

If you're using fabric strips as your loop material (Fig 8.1), cut the strips either on the straight grain or on the bias, depending on which gives you longer lengths; as a rough guide, cut the strips approximately 2.5cm (1in) wide for a canvas of 5hpi. However, if the fabric is very fine, you may have to cut the strips wider, in order to create enough bulk in the loop to cover both the locking thread and the canvas. If you're using yarn to create the loops, six-ply rug yarn would be suitable for a five-mesh canvas.

Fig 8.1

Locker hooks in two sizes

Equipment and tools

A locker hook resembles a large-eyed darning needle, but has a hook at the tip. Locker hooks are available in two sizes: a heavy-duty one for rug making, and a finer version for creating more detailed items on close-mesh canvases. In America, the method is worked by using two separate tools: a traditional rug hook, plus a lacing needle or bodkin for anchoring the loops. It's not essential to use a frame, although as the rug becomes heavier you may find that it's easier to handle if it's supported on a frame.

Design considerations

Fig 8.2

♦ As a regular-mesh canvas is used for the base, the completed rug tends to have a very linear appearance. As for needlepoint rugs worked on a large-mesh canvas, curved lines become stepped instead of rounded.

♦ It's not possible to achieve detailed pictorial shapes with this technique, as locker hooking by its nature relies on rows being stitched with a strip of fabric, rather than on individual stitches. It's much more suitable for simple, bold designs with large motifs and background areas, and is also particularly effective when it's worked in variegated, dyed yarns or fabrics.

♦ As with hand hooked and prodded rugs, cut strips of patterned fabrics, such as tweed, checks, florals and stripes, can create very interesting patterns and effects.

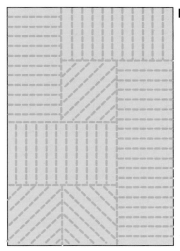

Fig 8.3

♦ You can introduce further textural interest by working the locker hooking in different directions, for example right to left, then left to right, thereby creating a slight herringbone pattern. It's possible to create more contrast still if you change the direction of the stitching by 90° in some areas (Fig 8.2), or work diagonally at 45° to the canvas mesh over some parts (Fig 8.3).

♦ To create a sculptured effect, you can try varying the size of locker needle you use or the thickness of the locking thread – or try winding the yarn or fabric strip twice around the locker hook to form each loop.

Working instructions

Use your preferred method (see page 14) to transfer the design to the canvas.

If you're going to finish the canvas edges later (see page 91), cover them with masking tape or binding before you begin work to prevent snagging.

Thread the locking thread through the eye of the locker hook. Hold a length of yarn or fabric on the underside of the canvas and, from the right side, push the hook end through the canvas; catch a loop round the hook and draw it up through the canvas. Move along to the next canvas hole, and repeat the process until you have several loops around the needle (Fig 8.4a). Then pull the needle, with its locking yarn, through the loops; this locks the loops onto the canvas (b).

Any ends of loop fabric or yarn can be left on the wrong side, to be covered later by a backing fabric. Each locking thread should be finished off by threading it through a few of the stitches on the wrong side.

Fig 8.4a

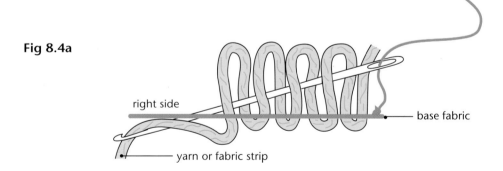

right side

base fabric

yarn or fabric strip

b

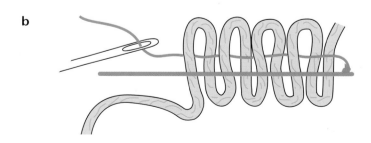

Finishing

If you prefer, you can neaten the edges of your canvas before you start hooking; turn them to the wrong side so that the stitching rows around the edges are worked through two layers of canvas. A 2.5cm (1in) allowance will be enough to make a very neat and secure edge. This method does mean, however, that you won't be able to attach the canvas to a frame for working, as you need a generous allowance around the working area to attach it to the frame.

If you're finishing the rug edges after you've finished the hooking, remove any protective tape, then turn the hems to the back and secure them with herringbone stitching. Cover this stitching with woven carpet tape, slip-stitching in position. Occasionally a tiny amount of bare canvas is visible at the edges of a locker-hooked rug; whip stitch is a neat method of covering the folded canvas edges (Fig 8.5). Use the same yarn or fabric as you've used for the loops, or work the whipping in a contrasting colour.

Adding a backing fabric is a good way of covering up the loop ends; however, the fact that the loops are locked in position means that you don't need to add a latex backing to stop the loops from pulling through.

Fig 8.5

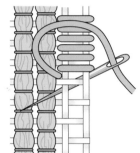

Variations

Blending two fabrics or yarns together in the needle produces an exciting variegated effect (Fig 8.6).

Try using a locking thread in a contrasting colour, in conjunction with loop fabric or yarn that's slightly finer than usual, so that the locking thread is partially visible (see the lower sample on page 87).

A braided edge around a locker-hooked rug creates an attractive textural contrast.

Instead of using a thick rug yarn or fleece, combine assorted strands of thinner yarn to make your loop thread; either use several colours of the same type of thread, or use a mixture of different shades and textures.

If you use a larger-count canvas, combined with a finer-loop yarn or fabric, you can create a smoother, less chunky texture.

Fig 8.6

LOCKER-HOOKED PROJECT
Rainbow-Striped Mat

MATERIALS
- 3.5hpi Zweigart canvas, 78 x 54cm (31 x 21½in)
- Assorted items of recycled clothing (or their equivalent in other yarns or fabrics); I used three navy and three black items, plus 20 other items (such as T-shirts, trousers, sweatshirts, shorts, jumpers and skirts) in assorted bright colours
- Thread in dark blue or black (six-ply rug wool is ideal, but thinner yarns can be doubled up), or approximately 5m (5yd) of fabric strips, cut 1cm (⅜in) wide
- Black calico or hessian for the backing, 78 x 54cm (31 x 21½in)

I created this mat entirely from discarded items of clothing. Mostly I used knitted fabrics, so that no fraying edges would be visible, although I also included a small amount of felt and cotton. The base colours were navy and black, with many bright colours randomly added. Most of the fabrics were plain, with a few patterned ones mixed in; this mixture of fabrics was particularly interesting to use, as the colours changed very quickly along each row.

FINISHED SIZE: 68 x 44cm (27 x 17¼in)

Working instructions

PREPARING THE FABRICS

First wash all the recycled garments, then cut them into strips approximately 2.5cm (1in) wide. (You may need to adjust this width slightly if any of the fabrics are particularly fine or thick.) Cut the strips as long as possible, stopping at the seam lines. As most of the fabrics I used were knitted, and so frayed edges weren't a problem, I cut the strips along the straight grain. If the fabrics you're using are likely to fray, cut them on the bias.

Fold over the top and bottom edges of the canvas and secure them with running stitch, so that you can work the locker hooking through a double layer of canvas on those edges to produce a neat finish. Work from top to bottom, and right to left. All the ends of the locking threads should be started and finished as for needlepoint rugs (see page 52); you can also start the fabric strips in this way, but the finishing ends will have to be secured later with a needle and thread.

An alternative is to join all the fabric strips beforehand, by hand or machine; this not only eliminates all the loose ends but also makes the locker hooking considerably quicker. However, this method does prevent you from making any choices about the positioning of specific colours as you work.

FINISHING

When you've finished all the locker hooking, turn under the raw edges of canvas at the edges of the rug, leaving one unworked canvas thread showing. Whip these (see page 141), using strips of the navy or black fabric in a very large-eyed needle.

Finally, make the tassels for the corners, using 1cm (⅜in) strips of all the fabrics (see page 140). Once the strips are cut, stretch them; the edges will either roll inwards, hiding the cut edge, or will stay stretched, forming an attractive wavy edge. Finally, back the mat with a piece of black cotton fabric, slip-stitched into position.

This detail of the mat shows some of the different fabrics used for the locker hooking

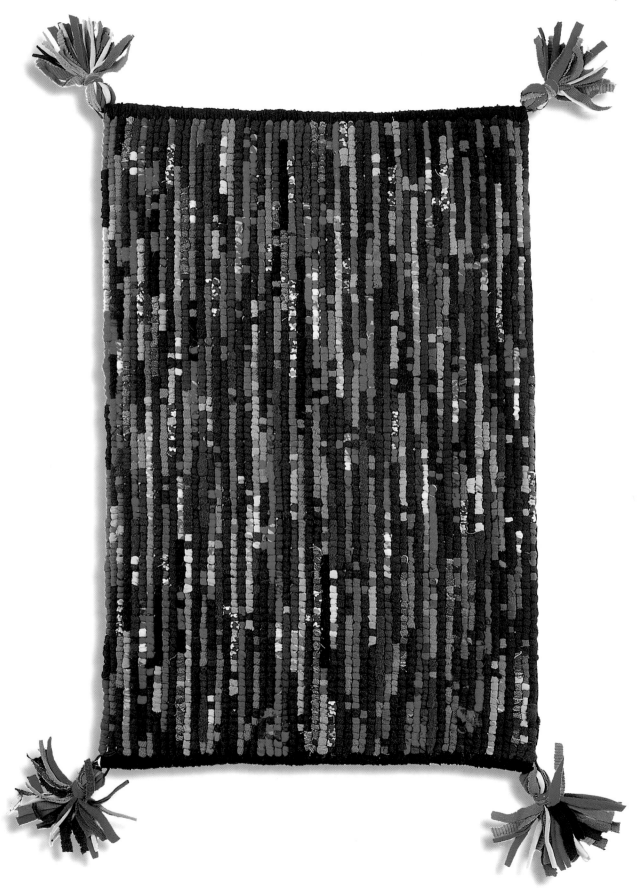

Tufted Rugs

CREATING A PILE with tufted knots is one of the oldest rug-making techniques of all; it was known in the second and third centuries in Persia and parts of the Middle East. The latch hook, a tool which can be used for creating the knots, is a twentieth-century development; it became very popular in the 1920s and 30s, because of its ease of use and suitability for home rug making. For many years now, rug companies have been selling kits for latch-hooked rugs consisting of printed canvases and pre-cut yarns. A version of the latch hook, including a spring to make the process slightly more automatic, was mentioned in *Weldon's Encyclopaedia of Needlework* published in 1939.

More recently, the hand-tufted rug has taken a new turn with the introduction of a tufting gun. This speeding-up of the tufting process, widely used in colleges and universities, has made it feasible for designers and artists to produce hand-tufted rugs commercially. Some rug makers have now established international companies creating pieces for both domestic and commercial interiors; others produce more experimental pieces, working to individual commissions – for example, Lynne Stein uses her electric tufting gun to combine rags with strings of beads and sequins.

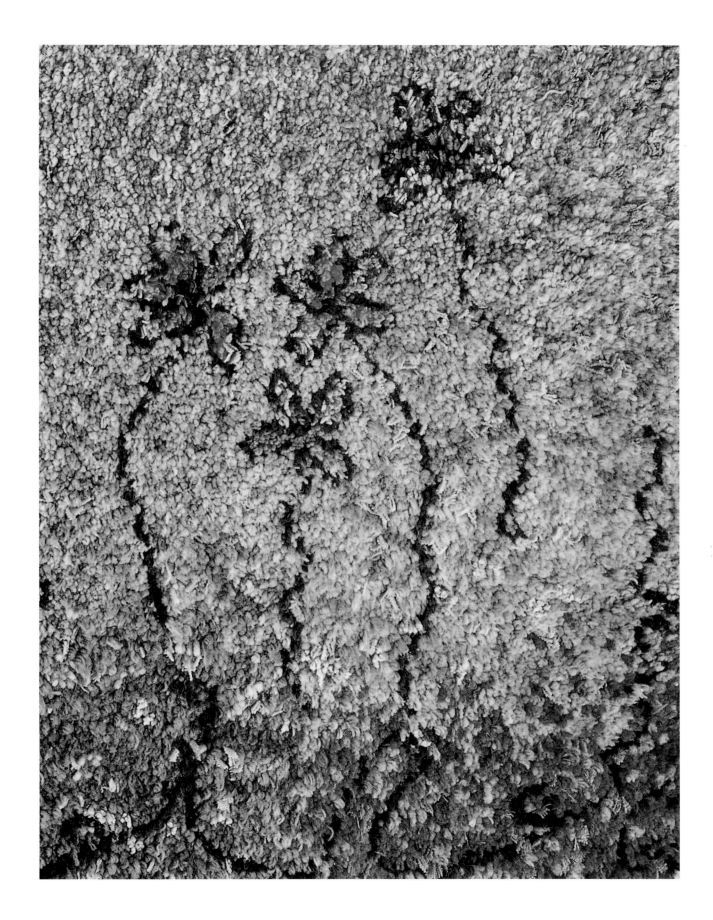

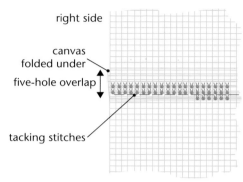

right side

canvas
folded under

five-hole overlap

tacking stitches

Fig 9.1

Fig 9.2

Materials and yarns

Canvas is used as the base fabric, so that the yarn or fabric strips can be knotted around the mesh. The standard size is 3.5hpi, for six-ply rug wool. As the maximum width of this canvas is normally 102cm (roughly 40in), you may have to join two widths for a full-size rug. If so, overlap the canvas pieces by five holes; line the holes up and tack the pieces together (Fig 9.1), then hook through the two layers when you reach that section. You can use hessian instead, but if you do you'll need to use the stronger (12oz) weight, and pull out every other thread to create a more open mesh for hooking onto.

Rug wool is available pre-cut to suitable lengths, but the pre-cut wools tend to have a rather limited colour range. Many people prefer to buy balls or hanks of six-ply wool, dyed or undyed, and then cut it to the required length; unfortunately, this kind of yarn is now becoming more difficult to obtain. The alternative is to use thinner wools or other threads, and combine two or more strands to make up the thickness you need. This, of course, produces a different textural quality as well as added colour interest. Weaving yarns are ideal for making tufted rugs, as they are very hard-wearing, but you can also select from a very wide range of novelty yarns (Fig 9.2). If you use these, however, they should be well mixed in with the tougher yarns, as they have a lower resistance to wear.

You can also include fabric strips in tufted rugs, but (as for prodded rugs) these should have a fairly close weave so that they don't break during the hooking process.

Equipment and tools

The latch hook (opposite page) has a wooden handle, a straight or curved stem, and a steel hook with a latch opening. A tufting gun can either be electric or powered by compressor. As each tuft punctures the canvas different pile heights can be produced, of cut or uncut loops; the gun can use either one yarn or several together, or fine fabric strips.

Design considerations

♦ There are interesting design possibilities with this technique, as each tuft is individually worked. This means that, if you wish, you can change the colour and texture of each tuft, producing very intricate designs.

♦ The design details are, however, very dependent on the length of the tufts produced. The average pile height for this method is 2.5cm (1in), using six-ply rug wool, and a pile of this length doesn't lend itself to intricate lines. When the pile is shortened to 0.75cm (⁵⁄₁₆in), using a finer yarn on a smaller-gauge canvas, there are many more design possibilities.

♦ Overall, this method is ideal for subtle colour changes and shaded backgrounds. The textural quality can be improved by combining different yarns and materials, varying the pile heights and hooking in different directions.

Working instructions

Preparing the tufting materials

Before you start, cut the yarn or fabric to the required length. As an approximate guide, the length of each strand should be twice the required height of the pile, plus an extra 2.5cm (1in) for the knot. If you're including fabrics in the design, these should be cut to a length of 6–12mm (¼–½in), depending on the thickness; if the fabric is fine, and needs to be folded double to create the required texture, the strips should be even wider.

Making the tufts

Work horizontally along each row rather than in colour blocks (as it will be difficult to fill in small unworked areas later), starting at the bottom of the design and moving upwards. All the knots should be made in the same direction, so that the pile lies in a uniform way (unless, of course, you're deliberately creating textural contrast).

The top of the latch hook opens and closes to allow the thread or fabric strip to be held secure

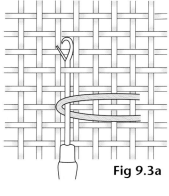

Fig 9.3a

Wrap the yarn around the hook shaft, and push the hook under one canvas thread (Fig 9.3a). Then take the two yarn ends through the open latch, and push them under the hook (b). Pull the hook towards you, until the latch closes around the yarn (c); continue pulling until the yarn ends are through the loop and form a knot (d). Tighten the knot by gently pulling both ends.

When all the hooking is completed, check the back of the canvas; it will be fairly evident if you've missed any stitches. If so, fill in the gaps.

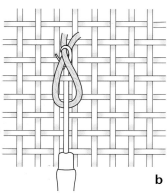

b

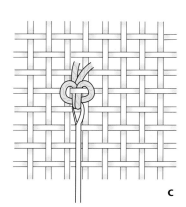

c

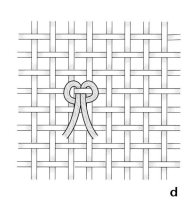

d

Finishing

You can make the hems around the canvas before or after you do the hooking, but whichever you choose it's best to protect the edges by attaching a carpet tape. If the rug is a curved shape, turn the edge under and snip the canvas before you work it, to ensure an even finish, then stitch the turning in place with a line of herringbone stitch (Fig 9.4).

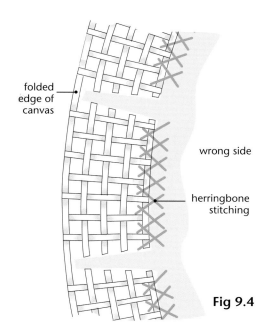

folded edge of canvas

wrong side

herringbone stitching

Fig 9.4

Variations

This technique is perfect for mixing different colours and types of thread and fabric, creating areas of subtle shading and interesting textures. Novelty dyeing, such as low-volume immersion, space- and tie-dyeing (see page 21), is an excellent way of creating fabric which will produce variegated effects when hooked (Fig 9.5).

Rya rugs are based on the rya or Ghiordes knot (see page 131), similar to the one created by the latch hook. There are several variations of this technique. One version uses a special Swedish backing canvas, which has weft threads already in position with gaps every 1.25cm (½in) for the stitches. The knots are usually worked with highly twisted two-ply rya yarn, using two, three or four strands together. A gauge is used to measure the pile length as each knot is made, and the loops can be cut afterwards if preferred.

Rya knots can also be made on a needlepoint canvas, either leaving a line unstitched every two or three rows, or stitching long-legged cross stitch (Fig 9.6) in between. These rows should be invisible between the looped ones, but as a safeguard it's best to work them in the same yarn (or one of a similar colour).

The pile height created by rya knots is longer than that created by latch hooking, usually 7.5–10cm (3–4in). If you combine strands of yarn that are varied both in colour and length, you can create a range of interesting effects.

Fig 9.5

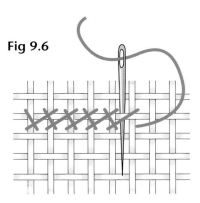

Fig 9.6

TUFTED PROJECT
FLOWERED RUG

MATERIALS
- Zweigart rug canvas, 3.5 holes per inch, 80 x 128cm (33 x 53in)
- Assorted yarns and fabrics for the knots. As a rough guide to quantities, this rug needs approximately 15,000 knots to cover the surface, of which there should be 550 dark navy, 700 dark blue, and 400 pink shades. Make these up from the following:
  - a variety of pre-cut Turkey rug yarn, in packs of 160 pieces
  - six-ply rug wool in hanks
  - two-ply weaving yarn, 80% wool, 20% nylon
  - natural-colour Norsk carpet yarn, hand-dyed
  - hand-dyed cotton, mohair, silk and linen threads
  - hand-dyed woollen blankets
- latch hook
- 4m/4yd of herringbone tape, 5cm (2in) wide

I've used the latch-hook technique to create a bright, contemporary design for this rug; the individual knots are made with separate pieces of fabric. This has enabled me to shade the colour areas within themselves, using various different types of yarn and some fabric, as well as mixing each colour subtly into the next area of the design.

The flower shapes were inspired by the work of the Bloomsbury group of artists, who delighted in portraying objects in a nonrealistic way. The colours gradually lighten from the bottom to the top of the rug – as do the outlines, changing from dark navy to a dark shade of blue, ensuring that they don't overpower the paler colours.

FINISHED SIZE: 72 x 120cm (roughly 30 x 50in)

Working instructions

PREPARATION
Remember to work in either metric or imperial throughout the project. Cut the canvas to size, then fold the 4cm (1½in) turning allowances to the wrong side. Keep these turnings in position by tacking along each edge.

To enlarge the pattern, draw the finished rug size on a large piece of paper, and divide it into 12cm (5in) squares, creating a grid of 10 by 6 squares. Now copy the pattern (Fig 9.8) from each grid square to the corresponding one on the paper. Make sure that your drawn lines are clear and bold, so that you'll be able to see them easily through the canvas mesh. Tape the canvas to the paper and trace the design, using a permanent marker pen.

Making the knots
Collect the yarns for one design area (select roughly 4–8 shades of one colour), and cut them into 7cm (2¾in) lengths. Cut the fabric first into long strips 1cm (⅜in) wide, then cut these into the short lengths ready for knotting.

Fig 9.7

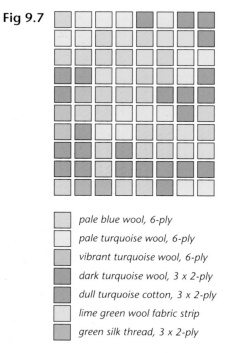

pale blue wool, 6-ply

pale turquoise wool, 6-ply

vibrant turquoise wool, 6-ply

dark turquoise wool, 3 x 2-ply

dull turquoise cotton, 3 x 2-ply

lime green wool fabric strip

green silk thread, 3 x 2-ply

In this detail of the rug you can see the length and density of the tufted pile, and the knots formed on the back of the work

Start latch-hooking the bottom row of the canvas, through the double thickness, and work across the row, rather than in blocks of colour; this helps to ensure that you don't miss knots. The shades in any one area can be varied as much or as little as preferred; as a guide, I worked a maximum of five consecutive holes with any one shade. Fig 9.7 shows an example of how the colours were varied.

Use the dividing lines on the pattern as a rough guide for the colour changes. These look best if each changeover is gradual, extending over approximately 5cm (2in) either side of the line, with occasional rogue knots further away. When you're using thinner yarns and threads than the six-ply rug wool, combine two or three yarns and hook them together. Continue hooking until all the holes have been filled.

FINISHING

Check on the wrong side for any missed knots; you'll easily be able to see any gaps, so fill these in using an appropriate colour. To give the edges of this rug added strength, slip-stitch a 5cm (2in) herringbone tape around the perimeter, folding the tape into a neat mitre at each corner.

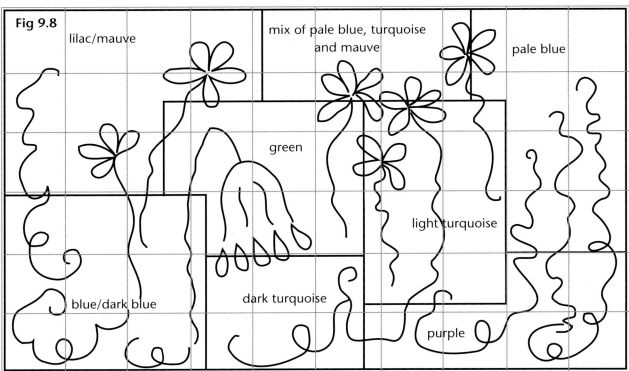

Fig 9.8

lilac/mauve

mix of pale blue, turquoise and mauve

pale blue

green

light turquoise

blue/dark blue

dark turquoise

purple

Knitted Rugs

The word 'knit' is derived from the Old English word *cnyttan* or *cnitten*, meaning 'knot'. There is evidence of knitting from prehistoric Peru, and the technique is thought to have been introduced to Britain by Spanish sailors wrecked off the Shetland Isles. *Mrs Beeton's Book of Needlework*, published in England in 1870, mentions knitting schools being established, and Queen Victoria's active encouragement of the technique.

The twentieth century has seen mixed fortunes for knitting. Machines have speeded up the process, while hand knitters have been inspired by novelty yarns and by designers such as Kaffe Fassett. Knitted rugs have never really been mainstream, as they are quite costly in yarn and cumbersome to work, but rugs using knitted fabric strips instead of yarn are an alternative that seems to be finding favour – especially with the renewed interest recently in rag rugs and recycling.

Materials and yarns

Knitted rugs are similar to woven rugs in that no base fabric or canvas is required. You can use a wide variety of materials for knitting, ranging from the types of fabric used for traditional rug weaving through to knitting wools, such as mohair, linen, cotton, synthetics, chenille and bouclé.

Obviously if you're knitting with yarns, these need to be of similar weights throughout the rug, or the surface will become bumpy and uneven. Fabric strips for knitting can also be made from various different materials (such as the cotton fabric used for the sample in Fig 10.1), but they should preferably be closely woven, or you'll find that numerous breakages will occur. Special finishes on fabric, such as glazing, strengthen the fibres considerably; the glazed chintz in Fig 10.2 was used to create the sample on page 107.

Fig 10.1

Fig 10.2

Equipment and tools

Knitting needles are the only tools required. These range in size from the maximum size 00000 (approximately 12mm, or ½in, in diameter), down to the very fine size 24. The maximum length is normally 35cm (14in), although circular needles are available up to 100cm (39in) long, which enables the knitter to make wider panels.

A 1960s English craft book mentions a knitting loom – a much-extended version of the cotton reel with nails used for so-called French knitting. This loom consisted of a length of wood, the same width as the rug, set with rows of nails. The yarn was wound around each nail in turn, then lifted over it with a crochet hook – basically a simple knitting machine.

Design considerations

♦ Knitting with yarn has enormous design potential, as we can see from the vast array of pictorial and textural patterns that are available. In knitting, as in needlepoint, individual stitches as well as rows can be varied to create exciting designs. Rag strips, however, aren't so versatile, as the stitches are much larger, but the large stitch becomes a feature itself.

◆ Complicated patterns would produce numerous fabric ends, or require strips of different colours to be carried along the row on the back of the work, both of which would be too bulky and messy. Instead, the design interest in knitted rugs comes not only from the structure of the stitches, but also from the use of patterned or different-textured fabrics.

◆ For extra interest, the fabric strips can be mixed with different yarns to produce varied textures in the finished rug.

Working instructions

Whether you're knitting with fabrics or yarns, a rug-sized piece of knitting would soon become too heavy and cumbersome – quite apart from the limitations imposed by the length of the needles. A much more realistic method is to knit sections; these are joined later with slip-stitching, using linen thread and a curved needle.

If you're knitting with fabric strips, these should be cut between 5mm and 1cm (roughly ¼–½in) wide; the exact size will depend on the thickness and closeness of the fabric weave, the size of the needles you'll be using, and the design detail that's required. Cut the lengths as long as possible, spiralling around a piece of fabric (Fig 10.3), then wind the lengths into balls. When you have to join two fabric strips for knitting, overlap the ends by approximately 1–2cm (⅜–¾in) and secure with a few stitches (Fig 10.4). If you prefer to knot the ends instead, make sure as you knit that the knots always lie on the wrong side of the work.

If you want to prevent your strips of fabric from fraying you can cut them wider, then turn the edges in as for braiding (see page 31). This is time-consuming, however, and can make the fabric strip very bulky to knit with. Different fabrics will fray by different amounts, but the problem of fraying can be reduced by cutting the strips on the bias. Once the strips are knitted up, the frayed edges soon wear away. It's always best to knit a sample first, to work out the number of stitches and rows your chosen material will produce per centimetre or inch; you'll find that the tension of knitted fabric strips is always much looser than when you're knitting with yarn.

Fig 10.3

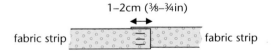

1–2cm (⅜–¾in)

fabric strip   fabric strip

Fig 10.4

Casting on

Make a slip knot and put it onto the left needle. Insert the right needle through the loop, wrapping the yarn round the right needle as shown (Fig 10.5a). Use the right needle to draw the yarn through the slip loop, to create a new loop over the right needle (b); pass this new loop back onto the left needle (c). Repeat until sufficient stitches have been created (d).

Fig 10.5a

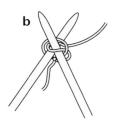

left   right

b

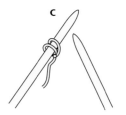

c

d

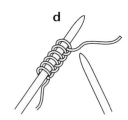

Plain knitting

Fig 10.6a

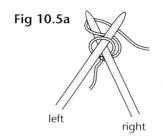

left   right

Insert the right needle through the first loop on the left needle, working from the left of the loop to the right, then wind the yarn round the right needle (Fig 10.6a). Use the right needle to draw a loop through the stitch as before; as you do this, slip the loop off the left needle (b). Continue along the row in the same way. Garter stitch is worked by using plain knitting for every row.

b

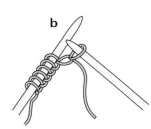

Purl knitting

Bring the yarn to the front of the work by looping it under the tip of the right needle. Insert the right needle through the front stitch, from the right to the left (Fig 10.7a), and loop the yarn round the right needle (b). Draw a loop of yarn through the stitch and onto the right needle, slipping it off the left (c). Alternate rows of knit and purl make up stocking stitch, and alternate stitches of knit and purl create a rib pattern.

Fig 10.7a

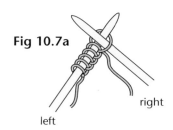

left   right

b

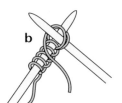

c

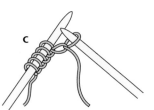

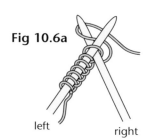

Casting off

Slip the first stitch of the row from the left needle to the right (Fig 10.8a). Work the next stitch, then lift the slipped stitch over the worked stitch and off the needle (b). Continue in the same way until all stitches have been removed. Slip the final stitch off the needle and thread the tail of the yarn through the loop to finish it off securely.

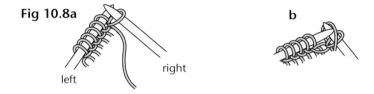

Fig 10.8a   left   right   b

Variations

Instead of knitting a rug in panels, it's possible to knit a long strip and wind it into a rug shape using the same method as for a braided rug (see page 30). Examples of rugs made this way, such as coiled and bull's-eye designs, have survived from the heyday of the Shakers in America. Alternatively, the knitting can be worked in wedge shapes then the wedges sewn together to make a circular or semicircular rug.

Knitted panels, or strips of knitting, look effective alternating with lines of latch-hooking, especially if you use fine yarns or long lengths for the hooking. Adding a crocheted border around a knitted rug provides an interesting contrast, as well as strengthening the joined sections.

Finishing

If you've worked the knitting in several pieces, a border will help to stabilize it. You don't need to apply a backing to a knitted rug, but if you do, especially if you also add an inner layer of felt or interlining, it creates a more padded and luxurious effect. An edging of carpet binding tape, stitched to the back of the rug, will help to strengthen the edges and, more importantly, will also reduce the rug's flexibility; this should enable it to maintain its shape.

Woven Rugs

WEAVING DATES BACK more than 20,000 years; one of the earliest known types of improvised loom used warp threads hanging from a tree branch, weighted with stones. By the Middle Ages treadle looms, which were operated by foot pedals, had been developed, and by the early nineteenth century the Jacquard system was in use. In this system, designs on punched cards are placed in the weaving machine, and produce both straight and curved patterns on the fabric automatically during the weaving process.

Weaving with fabric strips was eagerly adopted by early American settlers (as were the other rag rug techniques), and also developed extensively in Scandinavia. Today, commercial weaving takes full advantage of sophisticated computerized technology, but many people are also enjoying the revival in hand weaving. Enthusiasts can take advantage of the wide variety of looms available, a huge range of yarns, and an abundance of specialist classes and tuition.

Materials and yarns

A backing fabric is not necessary as the two sets of threads – the vertical warp and the horizontal weft – are woven together to form the rug. The warp threads need to be very strong, slightly elastic and relatively smooth. An ideal warp thread is high-twist and two-ply (that is, it's made from two separate threads twisted together firmly, which increases its strength), with a fibre content of 80% wool, 20% nylon, although many people making woven rag rugs favour a special warp cotton.

The strength of the weft is not so important, so a variety of fibres and fabrics, or both, can be used for creating the woven design. For very durable rugs which will receive a great deal of wear, it's best to use a traditional yarn of 80% wool, 20% nylon, or 100% wool, although silk, linen, cotton and synthetic threads provide interesting textures. You can also experiment with other materials such as cord, cane, raffia and plastic.

Fabric strips can also be used for weaving; these may be made of synthetic or natural fibres, and the fabric may be woven or knitted, patterned or plain. Fabrics such as tweed (Fig 11.1), velvet and Crimplene create interesting textures, while designs such as checks, stripes and florals produce intriguing patterns. If you cut the strips on the bias, this will reduce the number of frayed ends. However, if you do cut the strips along the straight grain, it's relatively simple to manipulate the edges inwards as you're weaving (Fig 11.2). Cut these strips as long as possible so that you don't have to make too many joins. The width of the strips will vary according to the fabric you're using; as a rough guide, cut thicker fabrics into strips 1.25–1.5cm (½–⅝in) wide, and thinner fabrics 2.5cm (1in) wide. If you do have to join fabric strips, stitch a cross-way seam on the sewing machine (see page 31).

Fig 11.1

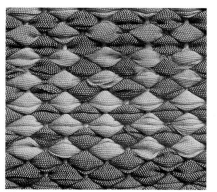

Fig 11.2

Long shuttles like these are used for carrying the weft

Equipment and tools

The main piece of equipment you need is a loom – simple or sophisticated. The simplest type of loom is a frame loom; these can be bought, or made fairly easily out of hardwood. The frame needs to be as strong as possible, so that you can create a firm tension on the warp threads, and so that you can beat the yarn or fabric quite hard against the work (see page 118). If you are making your own frame, insert rows of 7.5cm (3in) nails along the top and bottom edges, spacing them 1.25cm (½in) apart, with a second row staggered below (Fig 11.3). This gives an average of four warp ends (warp threads) per inch. Commercial looms range from small table ones, to massive 1.6m (63in) wide floor looms, and include many specialized features; these days many looms are computerized.

You will also need two shed sticks, slightly longer than the width of the frame. These are plain, flat sticks which are threaded through the warp threads; one under and over, the second over and under. When you turn each shed stick upright it lifts alternate warp threads to create a shed, or space, to allow the shuttle to pass through (Fig 11.4); for the reverse journey of the shuttle you turn the other shed upright, which lifts the other batch of warp threads. (On a commercial loom this process is carried out automatically.)

Shuttles (opposite page, below) are smooth lengths of wood, notched at the ends, although you can create improvised ones from strong cardboard; you will need one shuttle for each different colour you will be weaving.

A beater is a wooden and metal implement, used to beat each row of woven yarn and fabric close to the previous row so that the surface of the weaving is dense and firm.

1.25cm (½in)

Fig 11.3

Fig 11.4

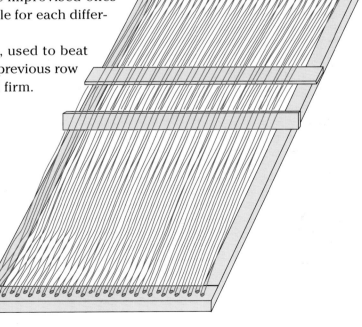

Fig 11.5

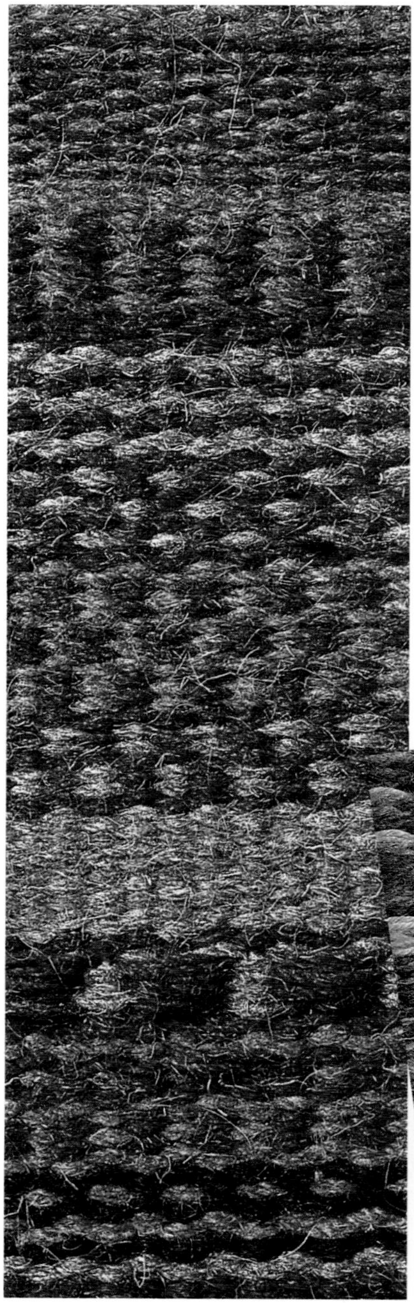

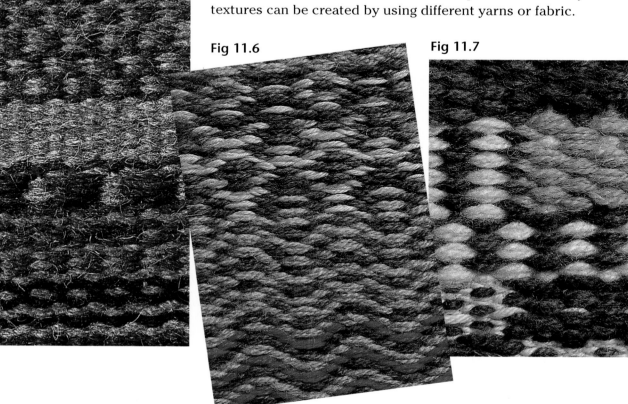

Design considerations

♦ Because of the linear nature of the weaving process, woven designs tend themselves to be linear and geometric. The simplest weave pattern is known as **plain weave** (Fig 11.5); this is produced by weaving over and under alternate threads on the first journey of the shuttle, and under and over the same threads on the return journey. There are numerous other weave patterns, such as **rib**, **padded rib**, **seersucker**, **double cloth**, **twill** (Fig 11.6), **herringbone**, **diamond**, **block** (Fig 11.7), **satin** and **crepe**. Many of these depend not only on different arrangements of the warp threads, but also on a multiple number of shafts – mechanisms which can lift small or large numbers of threads at one time to create different designs.

♦ A **warp-faced weave** is one where the warp threads are visible and completely hide the weft threads (Figs 11.8 and 11.9). In order to achieve this effect, you have to set the warp ends much closer together than for a weft-faced rug (the more usual effect, in which the weft threads are visible but the warp threads are not). Other textures can be created by using different yarns or fabric.

Fig 11.6

Fig 11.7

Fig 11.8

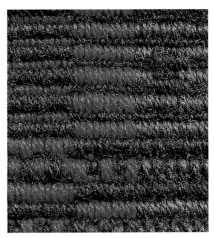

Fig 11.9

Working instructions

The strongest weaves are those where either the warp or the weft threads are dominant. If the weave is equally balanced between warp and weft the resulting fabric has too much flexibility and 'give' for a rug and may not lie properly flat; this kind of weave is more suited to fabric used for clothing.

If you're using a frame loom, tie the warp thread to the first nail, then wind it as tightly as possible from the top to the bottom of the frame and back until the whole frame is covered. It's advisable to use a double warp thread throughout, for extra strength, but certainly you must always use the thread double on the first and last two ends or nails, to create firm selvages – the finished edges of the woven piece.

The first task is to weave a heading (a trial band of plain weaving), 2.5–5cm (1–2in) deep, using the yarn or fabric you'll be using for the project. This process ensures that the warp is spread out evenly, and allows you to check that the weft is covering the warp well; it also provides a firm, straight base which supports the rest of the weaving. If you're working on a frame loom and want your finished rug to have a fringe, make your heading roughly 10cm (4in) deep, so that it can be undone and used to create the fringe when the weaving is complete.

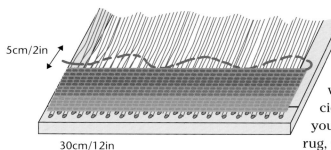

5cm/2in

30cm/12in

Fig 11.10

After you've completed each row of weaving, beat it down against the previous rows using a fork, a heavy comb, a beater or even your fingers to claw it down tightly. At intervals, the weft thread should be waved in a serpentine shape, so that the yarn is sufficiently slack to cover the warp threads. As a rough guide, you should do one wave for each 30cm (12in) length of the rug, with the top of the wave 5cm (2in) from the rest of the weaving (Fig 11.10). After you've waved the thread, beat it down as usual. When you're starting or finishing a length of yarn or a strip of fabric, weave the end into the work for approximately 8cm (3in or so), then leave the rest hanging at the back of the work, to be stitched in later.

Finishing

Once the weaving is finished, it must be cut off the loom; when you're cutting, make sure that you leave the warp ends (the plain warp beyond the weaving) long enough to knot or fringe if you need to. Woven rugs don't normally need either a binding or a backing fabric, but they do have warp threads at both ends which need finishing to prevent them from unravelling. The most common way of securing these is to finish them with overhand knots; the warp ends can then be darned away into the back of the rug, leaving a completely clean edge, or alternatively they can be left as a fringe.

To make the overhand knots take several warp ends (but no more than the number making up 2.5cm/1in of the warp), and tie them together (Fig 11.11), sliding the knot up to the edge of the rug and pulling it tight. Many rug makers prefer to make this fringe stronger by braiding, whipping or plying it, or by knotting it into a pattern (see pages 136 and 137), as in time it may wear away.

Fig 11.11

Variations

Inlay strips are an attractive design feature; they are laid on top of the pick (or line of weaving), under the warp threads, before the pick is beaten down. These strips can be made of coloured yarn, fleece, or strips of plastic or fabric (Fig 11.12).

A variation of inlay strips can be created with bows or rya knots (see page 131), which are part of a traditional Swedish technique called a **tatter weave**.

If you work one or more continuous rows of rya knots, this creates a pile effect which contrasts with the surrounding weaving (Fig 11.13). Before you work the knots, you need to close the shed space, so that the yarn or fabric can be knotted around two adjacent warp ends.

Fig 11.12

Fig 11.13

WOVEN PROJECT
STRIPED RUG

MATERIALS
- *For the warp:* two-ply, high-twist rug wool, 80% wool. 20% nylon, 600g (1½lb) in navy blue
- *For the weft:* two-ply rug yarn, 80% wool, 20% nylon, 150–200g (6–8oz) in each of 9 colours.

This is a plain-weave, or weft-faced, rug (see page 116) featuring stripes of nine colours: green, aqua, turquoise, purple, mauve, pink, red, blue and grey/blue. I based the design on the Fibonacci series of numbers, which relates to plant and animal structures; it's a formula that has been used by artists and designers for many years, either intuitively or consciously, as a means of arranging elements to achieve a balanced design. The numbers are the sequence 1 2 3 5 8 13 21 etc., each one being the sum of the two preceding numbers. In this design, the relative depths of the stripes correspond to the first five numbers of the series, but arranged in a random sequence across the rug.

I used a four-shaft Harris floor loom to weave the rug, but it could be created equally well on a hardwood frame loom, as described below.

FINISHED SIZE: 109 x 84cm (43 x 33in)

Working instructions

Fig 11.14

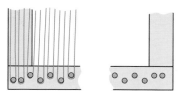

nails in each row: 70 + 1 extra

Use a simple frame loom, with nails placed in two staggered rows (see page 115), 1.25cm (½in) apart. As this rug has an even number of warp ends, the staggered rows will start and finish as in Fig 11.14. Add an extra nail 7mm (¼in) away from the last nail on each row; the warp end on each of these extra nails will be woven with the adjoining warp thread to strengthen the selvages.

Use three strands of two-ply yarn for each warp end, and attach the warp thread by tying a double slip knot round the first nail at one end. Now wind the yarn tightly round the first nail at the opposite end of the frame, continuing to and fro down the length of the frame until the last nail as shown; then fasten the warp thread securely.

Weave in the shed sticks, putting the first one under the first two warp ends (six strands of yarn), then over one warp end (three strands of yarn) and under the next until you reach the other side, finishing over the final two warp ends (six strands). Place the second

Fig 11.15a

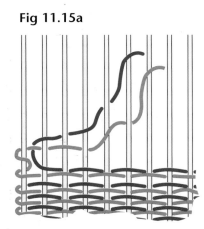

b

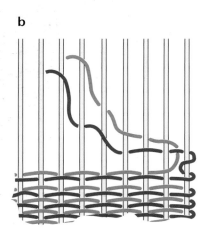

shed stick under and over the alternate warp ends from the first shed stick. (If you're using a floor loom to weave this rug, once the warp is made attach it to the back beam and thread it through the heddle eyes. Pass it alternately through the eight-dent reed, giving four ends per inch, and tie it tightly to the front beam stick. To strengthen the selvages, use six strands of yarn for the outer two warp ends on each side of the rug.)

On the chart opposite you'll see the colour sequence of the bands. Each stripe uses two colours: one colour from the previous stripe, together with one new colour. The bands across each main stripe in the design are created by weaving alternate rows, or picks, with the same colour.

Each weft row uses two strands of the two-ply yarn, making it the equivalent of four-ply. As you start or finish a colour, weave the ends in for a short distance (5–10cm/2–4in), splitting the strands for the last 1.5cm (½in) to lessen the bulk.

As you begin weaving, it's important to keep the selvages straight and the sides of the rug parallel. To prevent the edges from being pulled in, pull the weft thread really tightly around the last warp, but also pull outwards at the same time. Waving (see page 118) is also a key to keeping the width of the rug uniform.

As the total number of warp ends on this rug is an even, rather than an odd, number, this has the effect of creating different-coloured edges at each side of the rug. If there were an odd number of warp ends, the edges would be the same colour. You can probably see on the rug itself that within each stripe, each edge has only one colour showing and the other side has the other colour, rather than both edges having a mixture. This is achieved by wrapping the weft around the last warp (Fig 11.15a and b) on alternate rows.

FINISHING

When you've completed all the strips, having beaten down each row to create a strong, compact woven fabric, cut the warp ends from the loom and tie them across with overhand knots (see page 136). Thread each weft end through a large needle and sew it into the back of the weaving.

no. rows	start colour	end colour	no. rows	start colour	end colour	no. rows	start colour	end colour
16	blue	blue	6	grey/blue	red	8	turquoise	pink
40	pink	blue	20	grey/blue	turquoise	10	turquoise	purple
14	pink	aqua	6	green	turquoise	6	grey/blue	purple
26	purple	aqua	44	green	blue	20	grey/blue	green
18	purple	mauve	14	aqua	blue	6	red	green
10	turquoise	mauve	24	aqua	purple	8	red	aqua
34	turquoise	green	8	pink	purple	44	blue	aqua
4	red	green	12	pink	grey/blue	10	blue	purple
12	turquoise	green	4	pink	purple	18	turquoise	purple
8	grey/blue	green	14	pink	grey/blue	32	turquoise	mauve
14	grey/blue	purple	16	turquoise	grey/blue	8	pink	mauve
6	pink	purple	28	turquoise	blue	20	pink	green
44	pink	mauve	8	mauve	blue	6	grey/blue	green
6	aqua	mauve	28	mauve	green	20	grey/blue	purple
8	aqua	blue	4	pink	green	32	aqua	purple
6	green	blue	18	aqua	green	16	aqua	aqua
8	green	red	18	aqua	pink			

Other Techniques

THIS SECTION COVERS a group of lesser-know rug making techniques, and seems at first to be a rather diverse mixture. The section includes crochet, which dates back to the sixteenth century, and also weaving on a twentieth-century pegloom. One thing that unites all the techniques is that they are perfect for using recycled fabrics – in that sense, they are all variations on the basic technique of rag rug making.

Both crochet and appliqué stand in their own right as textile techniques; like needlepoint, knitting and weaving, they have been adapted for rug making as one of many applications. The example on the opposite page shows strips of fabric appliquéd using blanket stitch to create a rug design. In contrast, the pegloom, weaving sticks and shaggy strung methods are specialized techniques which are unlikely to be used for creating anything other than rugs. Increasingly we're seeing the boundaries blurred between 'rug' and 'non-rug' techniques, as designers experiment with small-scale hooking that is delicate enough for jewellery, and plastic strips and wires being woven, knitted and crocheted to create fabrics.

Pegloom

This is one of many modern basic frames or looms on which it's possible to do a simple form of weaving. In the late 1980s Wales hosted an exhibition of work produced on peglooms. The loom works on the basis of a yarn warp and a fabric-strip weft. One or more strong warp threads is cut for each peg, and threaded through the hole in the peg (Fig 12.1a). Fabric strips, either flat or folded in, are woven in and out of the pegs, each row alternating with the last (b). As the weaving grows, the pegs are removed one at a time and the warp threads pulled through. When the weaving is completed, the pegs are again removed so that the warp threads can be pulled through and tied. Each adjacent pair is knotted together, with the ends forming a fringe.

As an alternative to fabric strips the weft can be unspun fleece, a variety of yarns, old stockings and tights (pantyhose), or plastic carrier or refuse bags.

Fig 12.1a

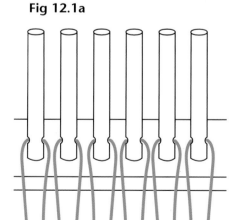

b

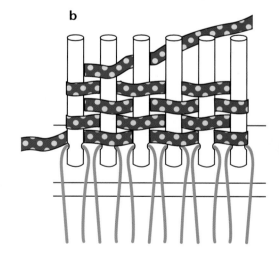

Weaving sticks

This technique has been used for many years in America, since the early settlers started their productive evening pastimes. Weaving sticks are used to create strips or squares of weaving that are later sewn together to form a rug or mat.

Five sticks are held at one time, and each has a strong warp yarn threaded through its hole; these are pulled through to the desired length, then the doubled ends are tied together (Fig 12.2a). The sticks are held in one hand and the weft thread in the other, then the weft is woven over one stick and under the next; it's looped around the last stick, then woven back across the row, alternating the 'unders' and 'overs' (b). When the sticks become full, they're gently eased up through the bulk of the weaving; this process is continued until the required length is woven. The work is finished off by tying the yarn end around the last stick and pulling all the sticks out from the work.

Fig 12.2a   **b**

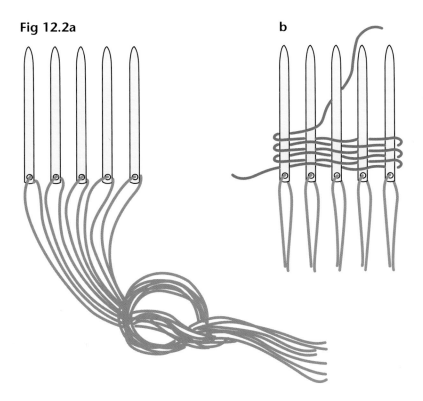

Crochet

Crochet is an old technique, used as early as the sixteenth century in convents to create decorative work; however, it's much more recently that it's been adopted as a rug-making technique. A 1920s British needlework magazine showed a rug featuring a crochet mesh filled with rag strips, and for a brief time during in the 1940s and 50s crocheted rugs had unprecedented popularity. Both yarns and fabric strips were used in a vast variety of patterns, and it's this use of fabric for crocheting that seems to have caught the imagination of rug makers today.

A complete rug can be made using only rows of double or treble chain stitches, the basic foundation stitches of crochet. These stitches can be worked in a spiral shape, or worked in rows to produce a rectangular rug (Fig 12.3). A variety of yarns are suitable for crochet, including rug wool, or a combination of thinner, textured threads. If the crochet is done with fabric strips, these should be cut approximately 2cm (¾in) wide and used unfolded; if they are cut wider, they'll be too bulky and the rug won't lie flat.

Fig 12.3

The finished effect is particularly pleasing when a patterned fabric is used. A quantity of approximately 1.5–2 metres (1½–2 yards) of cotton fabric would be needed for a 30cm (12in) square.

A rug crocheted in one piece can become extremely heavy so, as for knitting, it's a good idea to work the rug in sections, with the joins strengthened by a border. A lining is not recommended, as any dirt or grit will fall through the crocheted mesh and then be caught in between the layers.

For the combined crocheted and woven rug, an open or filet mesh is first worked into a base row of chain stitches (Fig 12.4). Fabric strips, approximately 9cm (3½in) wide, are folded as for braided rugs to eliminate raw edges, joined if necessary with a cross-way seam, then woven under and over the crocheted bars. The tension should be loose, so that the crocheted bars aren't pulled out of true.

Fig 12.4

Pieced appliqué

These rugs are derived from the 'pen-wiper' rugs of the late nineteenth century, when concentric circles of fabric – sold for cleaning the nibs of dip pens – were sewn onto a strong woollen background (Fig 12.5). The later 'penny' rugs were constructed on a similar principle, using circles of men's suiting, blanket-stitched onto a background. There were two other favourite shapes: a rectangle with two rounded corners, called a shingle or tongue rug, and a square patch – the design created from squares was called **layered blocks**.

Fig 12.5

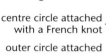

strong woollen background fabric

centre circle attached with a French knot

outer circle attached with blanket stitch

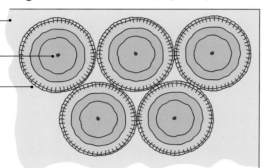

Today's appliqué rugs tend to resemble patchwork, with a variety of different-shaped pieces put together to form a pattern. Decorative hand stitching can be used, such as herringbone (see page 54), blanket stitch (Fig 12.6) and faggot stitch (Fig 12.7), or the patches can be joined with machine zigzag (Fig 12.8) or satin stitch. One designer, Rachel MacHenry, uses old woollen garments; first she felts them, then cuts them up, and secures the shapes onto a hessian backing with bonding web before stitching them in place. Of course felt is ideal for any appliqué work, as it eliminates the problem of fraying edges.

Appliquéd shapes can also be combined with other rug techniques such as needlepoint or hooking. When appliqué is combined with a technique that creates a thick surface, it's best to pad the shapes with carpet felt, curtain interlining, or woollen blanket. For hooking, the shapes are applied first, then the hooking is worked close to the edges. With needlepoint, which doesn't create such a strongly textured surface, the shapes are generally applied on top of the finished stitching.

Fig 12.6

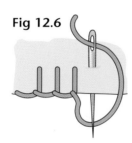

Fig 12.7

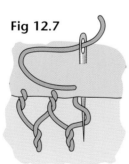

Fig 12.8

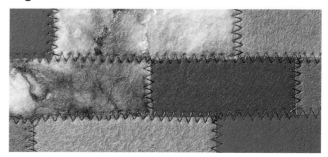

Shaggy strung or knotted

This is a rag rug technique currently popular in America. It uses short strips of fabric, similar to those used for prodded rugs (see page 64); the strips should be 8–10cm (3–4in) long, and 1.25–2cm (½–1in) wide. Each strip is tied over two warp threads, using a rya or Ghiordes knot (Fig 12.9a). The warp threads can be attached to pegs or nails, at opposite ends of a frame, and then the fabric pieces tied over alternating pairs (b); when all the knotting is complete, the knotted strips hold the rug together.

The other method of working this kind of rug is to attach two balls of string or yarn to nails or pegs on a board. The fabric pieces are knotted along the length of the strings, and moved along as they become full; when many strings are full of knots, they are then stitched (or knotted) together to create the rug.

Fig 12.9a
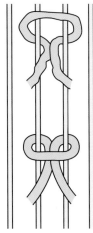
b
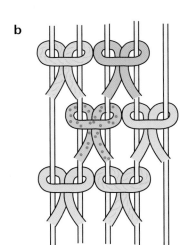

FINISHING
TOUCHES

Edges & Bindings

ONCE YOU'VE DESIGNED and worked your rug, the only thing left is to find the perfect edging or binding. I've already talked about bound and whipped edges (see pages 77 and 91), but there are numerous other ways of finishing a rug. When you're deciding on the best type of finished edge – or even whether to have one at all – there are various factors you'll need to take into account: for instance, the finished size of the project, the height of any pile, and the rug's structure, materials, texture, colour and design. Then choose an edging which suits from the ideas shown on the following pages.

Fibres

Fig 13.1

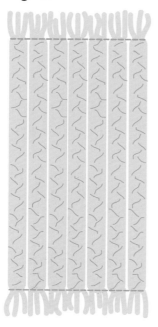

Woven rugs, whether they're made with wefts of yarn or of fabric, will all have warp ends that can be easily made into a fringe. Rugs worked on a woven base fabric, such as hooked, prodded and punch-needle rugs worked on hessian or monk's cloth, can either have the base fabric unravelled into a fringe or a separate one attached. If you want a fringe on a rug with a canvas base – for instance a needlepoint, tufted or locker-hooked rug – attaching a separate fringe is the only option. Rectangular braided rugs may already have fringes of fabric strips which just need securing with a line of stitching (Fig 13.1).

To finish off woven rugs, the warp ends are first secured with a row of overhand knots (Fig 13.2). This fringe can then be left, or you can add further decoration in various ways:

♦ You can create several rows of staggered overhand knots (Fig 13.3), using ends from adjacent knots in the preceding row. It's possible to devise many different knotting patterns (Fig 13.4), but if you want long, decorative knotted fringes remember to allow plenty of extra warp thread at each end.

Fig 13.2

Fig 13.3

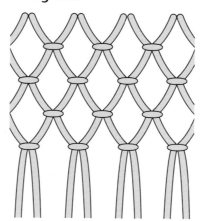

Fig 13.4

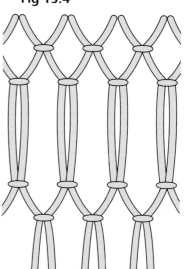

♦ For a variation on the double knot, the warp groups can be interwoven before tying a second row of knots (Fig 13.5).

♦ Multiple knots are created by tying a series of overhand knots down the length of each group of warp threads (Fig 13.6).

♦ Try alternating half-hitch knots down the length of each group of warp threads (Fig 13.7); this does, though, use up a great deal of warp thread.

Fig 13.5   **Fig 13.6** 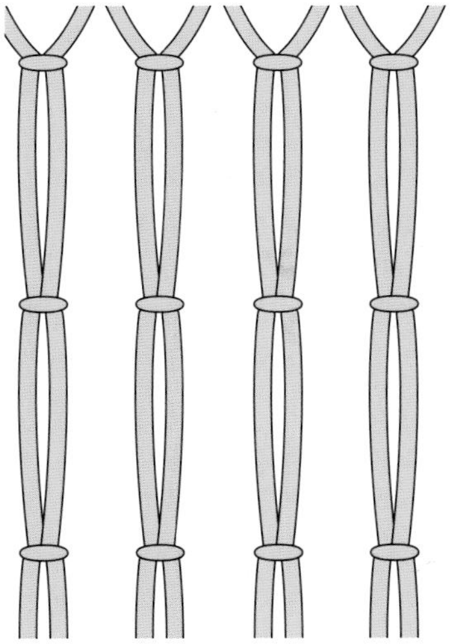   **Fig 13.7**

Fig 13.8   **Fig 13.9**

♦ Plying is a finishing technique which creates a fringe resembling thick cords. These are made by taking 6–12 threads, dividing them into two groups, and then twisting them together in the same direction as the yarn's natural twist. Finally the two groups are twisted together in the opposite direction (Fig 13.8), and finished with an overhand knot or whipping (see page 141).

♦ Needle-weaving, worked by weaving a needle in and out of groups of threads, can be used to gather the fringe ends, and also to create random patterns if you wish (Fig 13.9).

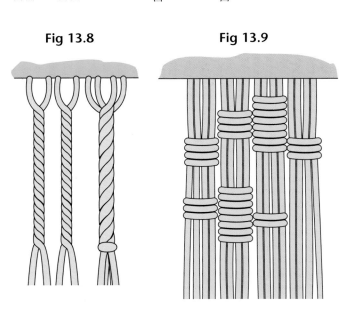

Fig 13.10

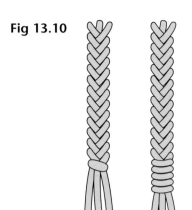

♦ You can make the fringe into a series of three-strand braids, each one finished by an overhand knot – or, if a knot is too bulky, by whipping (Fig 13.10). Alternatively, if the threads aren't too thick, you can create braids with four, five or six strands.

♦ Whipping is a neat way to finish several of the above methods, or it can be used effectively on its own, working the stitching in one long length or several smaller groups (Fig 13.11).

♦ If you require a fuller fringe, additional threads can be tied in with the initial row of overhand knots (Fig 13.12).

All these ideas for decorative fringe finishes can also be applied to separate fringes attached to hessian- or canvas-backed rugs, and to fringes created by fraying out woven backings such as hessian and monk's cloth.

To make a separate fringe, for knotting into a folded canvas or hessian edge, cut lengths of yarn twice as long as the finished fringe length plus 2.5cm (1in) for the knotting. Use a piece of card cut to size, wrap the thread around the card, then cut through the thread along one edge of the card (Fig 13.13). You can use the same yarn that you used for making the rug, or a contrast such as strong cotton or crochet yarn, a thick rug yarn, or several thinner yarns used together.

Fig 13.11

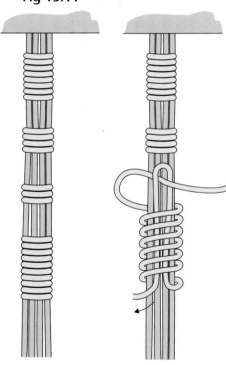

Fig 13.12

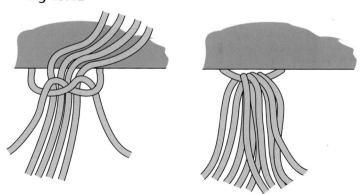

Fig 13.13

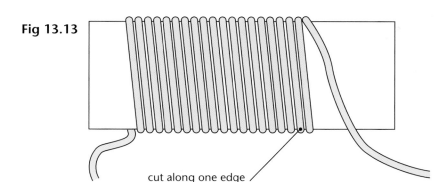

cut along one edge

On a canvas-backed rug, the fringe is attached through the first line of unworked holes. Insert the folded thread, and then pull the two ends through to form a neat knot (Fig 13.14). Repeat this along the entire row of holes, using a crochet hook or latch hook to speed up the process. If you're knotting onto a hessian edge, enlarge the holes in the weave first so that you can easily pass the fringe threads through them. If you're using a very thick fringing yarn, especially into a fine-weave canvas or hessian, use alternate holes only.

If you're unravelling hessian or monk's cloth to create your fringe, first secure the edges of the rug with a line of blanket stitch (see page 130) worked in linen thread. (It's often easier to carry this out before the rug is hooked, prodded or punch-needled.) Then fray the woven fabric by removing all the threads parallel with each edge of the rug. This method allows you to create a fringe on all sides of the rug – on woven pieces you can only fringe the two ends where the warp threads finish.

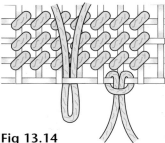

Fig 13.14

Tassels

You can include simple tassels in an attached fringe, or they can be added to the corners of a rug. You can use any yarn, or strips of fabric, to make the tassels, including a variety of novelty yarns and fabrics.

Depending on the length of tassel you require, wind the yarn or fabric strips around a piece of card or a ruler (see page 139); slide the threads off, then insert a separate thread through the loops at one end and tie it securely (Fig 13.15a). Approximately 1–2cm (⅜–¾in) from the looped ends, work about 1cm (⅜in) of whipping (b and c).

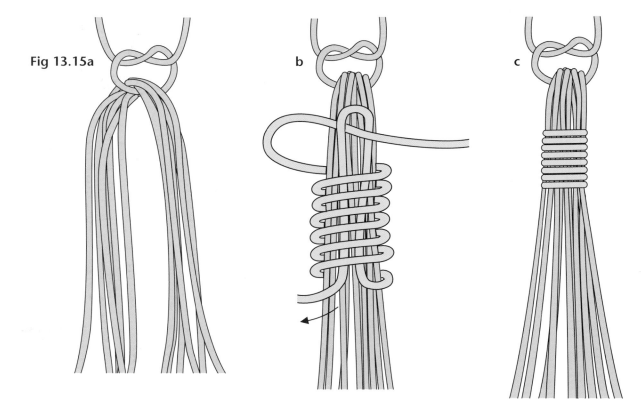

Fig 13.15a　　　　　　**b**　　　　　　**c**

Covered edges

These edgings are for canvas-based rugs, such as needlepoint, tufted or locker-hooked projects; you can work them with thick rug yarn, fabric strips with turned-in edges, or with multiples of thinner threads. Fold over the unstitched canvas edges; the number of threads you leave visible on the front will depend on the width of edging you want, but should be a minimum of two. These folded edges can then be finished in one of several ways:

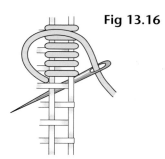

Fig 13.16

♦ Whip the edges, making several stitches in one canvas hole, depending on the thickness of the yarn and the canvas mesh size (Fig 13.16). Finish the ends of the whipping thread by threading them under several stitches at the back of the work.

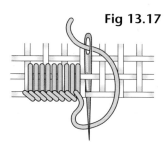

Fig 13.17

♦ Work blanket stitch or buttonhole stitch over the exposed edges (Fig 13.17).

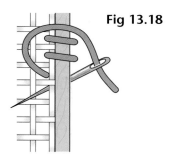

Fig 13.18

♦ Oversew a hand-made or ready-bought cord onto each canvas fold, building up a very firm edge (Fig 13.18).

♦ Create a plaited edge. This can be worked either by making three stitches forward and two back, or two stitches forward and one back (Fig 13.19a, b, c and d).

   With any of the above methods you could pad the canvas first by laying lengths of rug wool along the weave; this ensures that no speck of canvas shows through the stitching. Each of these methods could also be worked before the rug is stitched or hooked, although this does then mean that the canvas can't be attached to a frame.

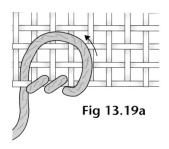

Fig 13.19a

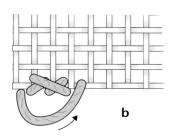

b

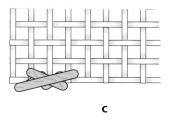

c

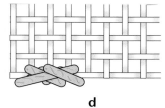

d

Shaped fabric edges

Shaped edges are suitable for hooked and prodded rugs; they are created from fabric, then machine-stitched to the hessian backing before the rug design is worked. Make a template of your chosen shape, and cut two fabric pieces for each side of the rug, adding a 1.5cm (⅝in) seam allowance on each edge. Place the two pieces of fabric right sides together, and machine around, leaving the straight edge open (Fig 13.20). Turn to the right side, press the edging flat, then machine-stitch each border to the hessian. If these fabric pieces seem a little thin compared to the rug, you can include a little padding when you're making up the shapes. Triangles and scallops are very suitable shapes, and can easily be overlapped for more interesting variations (Fig 13.21).

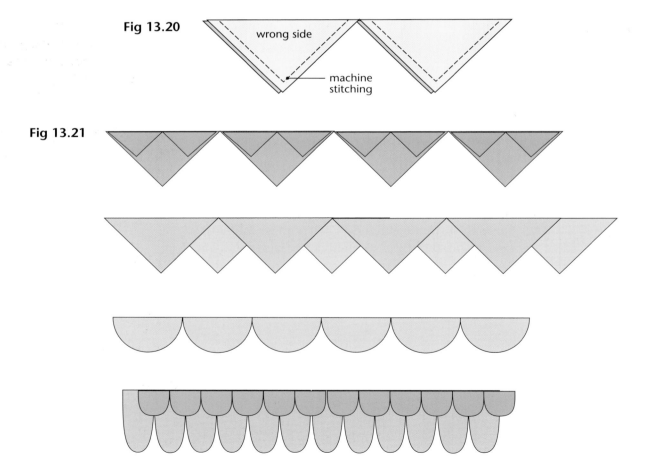

Fig 13.20

wrong side

machine stitching

Fig 13.21

Glossary

Acetic acid
A chemical solution, used in the form of vinegar with acid dyes

Acid dye
A type of dye which uses acetic acid and sodium sulphate to fix the colour

Adjacent colour scheme
One based on adjoining colours in the colour wheel

Anchored loop
American term for locker hooking

Aniline dyes
Chemical dyes used for fabric and yarn

Base fabric
Sturdy fabric, such as hessian or canvas, often used as the foundation for certain rug-making techniques

Beater
Tool used to beat a row of weaving tightly against previous rows

Blocking
The process of ensuring that the grain and edges of a piece of needlepoint are straight

Burlap
American name for hessian

Canvas
An evenly woven mesh used as a base fabric for some rug techniques

Carding
The process of combing fleece to remove knots and tangles

Carpet shears
Another name for napping scissors

Cartoon
Full-size drawing of a proposed design

Cloth stripper
Machine which cuts even strips of cloth

Colour wheel
Diagram displaying the colours of the spectrum in a circle

Complementary colours
Two colours that appear opposite each other on the colour wheel

Contour hooking
A method of hooking which echoes shapes or irregular lines

Discharge methods
Techniques for removing the pigment from certain areas of coloured fabric

Disperse dye
A type of dye which uses heat to fix the colour

Double canvas
A type of canvas woven from pairs of threads

Eggbeater
Another name for a *tappenalen*

Fibre-reactive dye
A type of dye which uses an alkali to fix the colour

Fleece
Sheep's wool

Glauber's salt
Sodium sulphate, a chemical salt used with acid dyes

Heading
A section of plain weaving worked at the start of a design

Herringbone tape
Sturdy tape used for neatening the edges and backs of rugs

Hessian
A rough, loosely woven cloth used as a base fabric for some rug techniques

Hpi
Abbreviation of 'holes per inch,' used to describe canvas mesh sizes

Interlock canvas
A type of canvas woven from twisted threads

Locking thread
Fine thread used to anchor the loops in locker hooking

Loom
Frame used for weaving

Monk's cloth
Strong fabric which can be used as the base fabric in some rug-making techniques

Mono canvas
A type of canvas woven from single threads

Mono de luxe canvas
A heavy-duty canvas especially useful for rug making

Monochromatic colour scheme
One based on shades and tints of one colour

Mood board
Collection of samples based on one topic, colour scheme or inspiration

Napping scissors
Large shears used for trimming the loops of hooked rugs

Natural dyes
Pigments derived from animal, plant or mineral sources

Natural fibres
Those derived from animal or plant sources – for instance cotton, wool, silk, linen

Over-dyeing
Dyeing an assortment of fabrics or yarns with a single colour to unify their tones

Pick
A single row of weaving

Plain weave
Basic over-and-under weaving pattern

Platform cloth
A strong fabric used for backing rugs

Prodder
Smooth-tipped tool used for creating prodded rugs

Punch needle
A mechanized tool used for hooking rugs

Resist
Any substance used to protect certain parts of a fabric or yarn from taking up pigment during dyeing

Rya knot
A type of knot used in some rug-making techniques

Selvage (or selvedge)
Firm woven edge of a fabric

Shed
Space created in weaving for a shuttle to pass through

Shed stick
Narrow length of wood, used in pairs to create a shed when weaving

Shuttle
Long, notched piece of wood used to carry weft threads

Shuttle hook
Another name for a speed hook

Speed hook
A mechanized tool for hooking rugs

Staple
Term used to describe the length of fibres in a fleece

Sudan canvas
A large-hole canvas particularly suitable for rug making

Synthetic fibres
Chemically-produced fibres – for example acrylic, nylon and polyester

Tapestry needle
Type of needle with a blunt tip, particularly for use on canvas

Tappenalen
Danish tool for hooking rugs

Tatter weave
A design in which rya knots are interspersed with weaving

Tops
Ready-prepared and dyed fleece used for felting

Tramming
Long straight stitches worked across canvas before working decorative stitches

Warp
The vertical threads in a piece of weaving

Warp cloth
Another name for monk's cloth

Warp cotton
Strong thread used for warping looms

Warp-faced weave
One in which the warp threads show and the weft does not

Weft
The horizontal threads in a piece of weaving

Weft-faced weave
One in which the weft threads show and the warp does not

Index

Acknowledgements

The author would like to thank the following companies, suppliers of specialist yarns and materials:

Atlascraft CAS Group, PO Box 12, Saxmundham, Suffolk IP17 3PB, England (tel 01728 648717)

DMC Creative World Ltd., Pullman Road, Wigston, Leicestershire LE18 2DY, England (tel 01162 811040)

Fibrecrafts, Old Parsonage Road, Peasmarsh, Guildford, Surrey GU7 2QD, England (tel 01483 565800)

Readicut Wools (The Craft Collection Ltd), Terry Mills, Ossett, West Yorkshire WF5 9SA, England (tel 01924 275246)

Texere Yarns, College Mill, Barkerend Road, Bradford, West Yorkshire BD1 4AU, England (tel 01274 722191)

The Handweavers' Studio & Gallery Ltd., 29 Haroldstone Road, London E17 7AN, England (tel 0208 5212281)

Omega Dyes, Prescott House, Old Hill, Longhope, Gloucestershire GL17 0PE, England (tel 01452 830496)

About the author

SANDRA HARDY was born in Cheshire, England, but for many years has lived in rural Berkshire with her husband and three daughters. As a child she spent many happy hours trying out various crafts and different kinds of stitching. However, this was all put to one side while she studied Social Sciences at university, then pursued a career in personnel management.

She later took a City & Guilds further education course in Soft Furnishings, Upholstery and Design, and soon became involved in creating needlepoint projects for stitching magazines. Since then her craft work has diversified to include blackwork, beadwork, appliqué, quilting, cross stitch and machine embroidery as well as rug making. Her first rug was a needlepoint design with floral panels and borders, stitched for Future Publishing's *Needlecraft* magazine. Since then she has created rugs in many different techniques.

Sandra is the author of several books, including the extremely popular *Needlepoint: A Foundation Course,* also published by GMC Publications. She combines her writing work with teaching adults, both locally and at national stitching exhibitions and fairs.

Titles available from
GMC Publications

BOOKS

Crafts

American Patchwork Designs in Needlepoint *Melanie Tacon*
A Beginners' Guide to Rubber Stamping *Brenda Hunt*
Blackwork: A New Approach *Brenda Day*
Celtic Cross Stitch Designs *Carol Phillipson*
Celtic Knotwork Designs *Sheila Sturrock*
Celtic Knotwork Handbook *Sheila Sturrock*
Celtic Spirals and Other Designs *Sheila Sturrock*
Collage from Seeds, Leaves and Flowers *Joan Carver*
Complete Pyrography *Stephen Poole*
Contemporary Smocking *Dorothea Hall*
Creating Colour with Dylon *Dylon International*
Creative Doughcraft *Patricia Hughes*
Creative Embroidery Techniques Using Colour Through Gold
Daphne J. Ashby & Jackie Woolsey
The Creative Quilter: Techniques and Projects
Pauline Brown
Decorative Beaded Purses *Enid Taylor*
Designing and Making Cards *Glennis Gilruth*
Glass Engraving Pattern Book *John Everett*
Glass Painting *Emma Sedman*
Handcrafted Rugs *Sandra Hardy*
How to Arrange Flowers: A Japanese Approach to English
Design *Taeko Marvelly*
How to Make First-Class Cards *Debbie Brown*
An Introduction to Crewel Embroidery *Mave Glenny*
Making and Using Working Drawings for Realistic Model
Animals *Basil F. Fordham*
Making Character Bears *Valerie Tyler*
Making Decorative Screens *Amanda Howes*
Making Fairies and Fantastical Creatures *Julie Sharp*
Making Greetings Cards for Beginners *Pat Sutherland*
Making Hand-Sewn Boxes: Techniques and Projects
Jackie Woolsey
Making Knitwear Fit *Pat Ashforth & Steve Plummer*
Making Mini Cards, Gift Tags & Invitations *Glennis Gilruth*
Making Soft-Bodied Dough Characters *Patricia Hughes*
Natural Ideas for Christmas: Fantastic Decorations
to Make *Josie Cameron-Ashcroft & Carol Cox*
Needlepoint: A Foundation Course *Sandra Hardy*
New Ideas for Crochet: Stylish Projects for the Home
Darsha Capaldi
Patchwork for Beginners *Pauline Brown*
Pyrography Designs *Norma Gregory*
Pyrography Handbook (Practical Crafts) *Stephen Poole*

Ribbons and Roses *Lee Lockheed*
Rose Windows for Quilters *Angela Besley*
Rubber Stamping with Other Crafts *Lynne Garner*
Sponge Painting *Ann Rooney*
Stained Glass: Techniques and Projects *Mary Shanahan*
Step-by-Step Pyrography Projects for the Solid Point
Machine *Norma Gregory*
Tassel Making for Beginners *Enid Taylor*
Tatting Collage *Lindsay Rogers*
Temari: A Traditional Japanese Embroidery Technique
Margaret Ludlow
Theatre Models in Paper and Card *Robert Burgess*
Trip Around the World: 25 Patchwork, Quilting
and Appliqué Projects *Gail Lawther*
Trompe l'Oeil: Techniques and Projects *Jan Lee Johnson*
Wool Embroidery and Design *Lee Lockheed*

Dolls' Houses and Miniatures

1/12 Scale Character Figures for the Dolls' House
James Carrington
Architecture for Dolls' Houses *Joyce Percival*
The Authentic Georgian Dolls' House *Brian Long*
A Beginners' Guide to the Dolls' House Hobby *Jean Nisbett*
Celtic, Medieval and Tudor Wall Hangings in 1/12 Scale
Needlepoint *Sandra Whitehead*
The Complete Dolls' House Book *Jean Nisbett*
The Dolls' House 1/24 Scale: A Complete Introduction
Jean Nisbett
Dolls' House Accessories, Fixtures and Fittings
Andrea Barham
Dolls' House Bathrooms: Lots of Little Loos *Patricia King*
Dolls' House Fireplaces and Stoves *Patricia King*
Dolls' House Window Treatments *Eve Harwood*
Easy to Make Dolls' House Accessories *Andrea Barham*
Heraldic Miniature Knights *Peter Greenhill*
How to Make Your Dolls' House Special: Fresh Ideas
for Decorating *Beryl Armstrong*
Make Your Own Dolls' House Furniture *Maurice Harper*
Making Dolls' House Furniture *Patricia King*
Making Georgian Dolls' Houses *Derek Rowbottom*
Making Miniature Food and Market Stalls *Angie Scarr*

Upholstery

Woodcarving

Woodturning

Woodworking

Toymaking

Photography

Gardening

VIDEOS

Drop-in and Pinstuffed Seats	*David James*	Twists and Advanced Turning	*Dennis White*
Stuffover Upholstery	*David James*	Sharpening the Professional Way	*Jim Kingshott*
Elliptical Turning	*David Springett*	Sharpening Turning & Carving Tools	*Jim Kingshott*
Woodturning Wizardry	*David Springett*	Bowl Turning	*John Jordan*
Turning Between Centres: The Basics	*Dennis White*	Hollow Turning	*John Jordan*
Turning Bowls	*Dennis White*	Woodturning: A Foundation Course	*Keith Rowley*
Boxes, Goblets and Screw Threads	*Dennis White*	Carving a Figure: The Female Form	*Ray Gonzalez*
Novelties and Projects	*Dennis White*	The Router: A Beginner's Guide	*Alan Goodsell*
Classic Profiles	*Dennis White*	The Scroll Saw: A Beginner's Guide	*John Burke*

MAGAZINES

WOODTURNING • WOODCARVING • FURNITURE & CABINETMAKING
THE ROUTER • WOODWORKING • THE DOLLS' HOUSE MAGAZINE
WATER GARDENING • OUTDOOR PHOTOGRAPHY
BLACK & WHITE PHOTOGRAPHY
BUSINESS MATTERS

The above represents a full list of all titles currently published or scheduled to be published.
All are available direct from the Publishers or through bookshops, newsagents and specialist retailers.
To place an order, or to obtain a complete catalogue, contact:

GMC Publications,
Castle Place, 166 High Street, Lewes, East Sussex BN7 1XU, United Kingdom
Tel: 01273 488005 Fax: 01273 478606
E-mail: pubs@thegmcgroup.com

Orders by credit card are accepted